Baudelaire

Baudelaire

by M. A. RUFF

translated and slightly abridged by
AGNES KERTESZ

NEW YORK UNIVERSITY PRESS 1966

LIBRARY OF CONGRESS CATALOG CARD NUMBER: 65–10767
MANUFACTURED IN THE UNITED STATES OF AMERICA

The original French edition of this book appeared under the title BAUDELAIRE *and was published by Hatier, Paris, in that company's "Connaissance des Lettres" series.*

CONTENTS

Baudelaire

1 · *The Innocent Paradise*

GREAT AREAS of shadow still remain in the Baudelairean field, and it is to be feared that no amount of research will ever succeed in clarifying them completely. If the only resulting inconvenience were that of leaving too great a margin to the reader's imagination with regard to Baudelaire's works, there would not be too much cause for distress, for the poet himself demands that a work of art open "profound avenues to the most adventurous imagination." Unfortunately, the imagination of his biographers has also had free play. The poet took pleasure in covering up his tracks, both because he felt that "profound feelings possess a purity which forbids transgression," and because "his diabolical taste for the ridiculous permitted him to take particular pleasure in the travesties of slander."

Each generation of critics has deposited a new layer of alluvial ground, and the labors of the disinterested scholar resemble those of archaeologists engaged in unearthing a city buried under successive deposits. The only means of recapturing the truth is to confine oneself to authentic documents, and to subject the testimony of Baudelaire's contemporaries and even of his intimate friends to an extremely rigorous critical examination. The Baudelaire that one discovers by this process differs acutely from the one whom tradition has preserved for us.

Charles-Pierre Baudelaire was born in Paris on April 9, 1821, of a mother who, on September 19, 1819, at the age of twenty-six, had married a man of sixty. Her history is not unique, and was not even unusual in earlier times. To draw from it conclusions of a physiological nature would perhaps be inadvisable. We should note instead that our poet came into the world with a heredity encumbered on both sides: his half-brother, Alphonse Baudelaire, the issue of his father's earlier marriage, died in 1862 of a cerebral hemorrhage with hemiplegia of the left side, and his mother herself died an aphasic as her son Charles had done before her. It is unnecessary, therefore, to concern ourselves with his youthful indiscretions, though they no doubt occurred.

We know very little about the paternal and maternal ancestry of the poet. His father, born in 1759 in a small commune of the Canton of Sainte-Menehould, came from a simple family of vine growers and farmers from Champagne. He himself was the result of a late marriage, and Baudelaire had a grandfather who was born under the reign of Louis XIV, in 1711. Joseph-François Baudelaire, the poet's father, was undoubtedly a gifted man. He was given a good education, entered the seminary, and, as his son stated several times without being believed, he was very probably ordained a priest. One should note that he belonged to the Châlons diocese, the most active Jansenist center in the kingdom. After having served as assistant master at the Collège of Sainte-Barbe, he entered the household of the Duke of Choiseul-Praslin as tutor to his children, and led a most pleasurable life in good society. Being a great art lover as well as a dabbler in painting, he associated with the artists of his generation, among them the sculptor Ramey, and the painters Naigeon and Prudhon. We can believe that his mind did not lack distinction, as he was received in the salon of Madame Helvétius, where he came to be a friend of Condorcet and Cabanis.

During the Revolution he spared no efforts on behalf of his friends, and aided his benefactors, the Choiseul-Praslins, who eventually supported the Empire and found themselves in high favor. They in their turn then gave proof of their gratitude by securing for him a respected and profitable position in the Senate administration. There he was respected by prominent men, and he fulfilled to the last all expectations concerning his merits. He seems to have considered his bureaucratic functions as mere sources of revenue, as a "secondary occupation," for though they are mentioned on the birth certificate of the poet, the baptismal record refers to Joseph-François as simply a painter. The same designation appears on the certificate of marriage to his first wife, Rosalie Janin, whom he married in 1797 and who left him a widower in 1814. He was obliged to defrock at the time of this marriage, but the Church did not withhold pardon from priests who had married during the Revolution.

When his former pupil, a bit too eager to change sides in 1814 and 1815, fell into temporary disfavor, he was placed on the retired list. His resources had expanded because of the savings he had invested during the First Empire, and an annuity provided by the Choiseul-Praslins, and he was still leading a comfortable life when he married Caroline Archenbaut-Defayis, a penniless orphan, in 1819.

Baudelaire was only six years old when his father died, yet he retained recollections of him which grew in importance with the passage of time. They stamped his personality more profoundly than one can easily believe, with a mark which nothing effaced. This father, who had conserved the mannerisms, expressions, and the tastes of the eighteenth century, also passed them on to his son. Except for school memories, this is what he remembered most from his childhood: "Old Louis XVI furniture, antiques, consulate period, pastels, eighteenth century society." His extreme politeness, which struck everyone with whom he came in contact, and which was sometimes erroneously mistaken for affectation, was doubtlessly bequeathed him by this eighteenth century to which his thought was bound.

Baudelaire also derived his "taste, which has lasted since childhood, for all the plastic arts" from his father, who had been a great dauber of canvas and frequenter of salons. A sculptor and a painter were summoned as witnesses when he was born, and his entire childhood was shaped by the "worship of pictures, his great, his unique, his earliest passion."

Through her letters and other people's evidence, we learn a great deal about the character of his mother Caroline, who survived her son and did not die until 1871. Little is known of her origins except that she was born in London in 1793, of a father who seems to have been an officer and an *émigré*. Several years later we find her in Paris, where she was taken into the protection of a barrister upon the death of her mother in 1800. This barrister, Pierre Pérignon, who became a baron under the Empire, was a childhood friend of Joseph-François Baudelaire. The latter had therefore known Caroline since her childhood, long before he could have contemplated marrying her. Pérignon, whose family was represented in Parliament and who had been tonsured at Sainte-Menehould, had received and had probably transmitted to his pupil, a religious education with Jansenist leanings. Joseph-François Baudelaire, whatever his religious ideas were at the time, found a similar spiritual disposition in his young wife.

The first years of the poet were an "innocent paradise," the delights of which he later recalled more than once with inconsolable nostalgia. It is difficult to determine the extent to which this happiness was upset by the death of his father in 1827. It seems that Caroline, susceptible to the prestige of social connections and of the trappings of luxury, had become attached to the affable old gentleman in spite of the difference in their ages.

But her grief was neither profound nor lasting, and it is likely that after a few days of mourning the six year old child was won over entirely by the tenderness which his mother lavished upon him. The days which they spent together in the little house at Neuilly remained one of his clearest and dearest memories:

> I have never forgotten, close to the town,
> Our white house, small and tranquil . . .

Twenty months later, however, his mother married Major Aupick, a brilliant officer only four years her senior, and this time it was a marriage for love. Whatever has been said, even by Baudelaire himself, it is quite likely that at the time the child did not experience a hostile reaction to the marriage. His relations with his stepfather appear to be warm and cordial until his eighteenth year, and his behavior does not disclose any hidden wounds. Had it not been for the incompatibility of temperament which then came to the fore, one may suppose that Baudelaire would not have felt any resentment of this second marriage, which endowed his mother with a comfortable, and even a flourishing, existence. But in his later bitterness he blamed his stepfather as the first source of his sorrows, and both legend and psychoanalysis have succeeded in blurring our perspective.

It is important to re-establish this perspective if we are to understand Baudelaire's mind and the genesis of his art. We must not prematurely pin a Satanic smile upon this self-styled "nice boy"—this little twelve year old man "who never missed a single quadrille," and whom his friends found "always affectionate," and blessed with a "soul at once delicate, refined, inventive, and tender." No doubt the atmosphere at the familial hearth was a little austere. No doubt Major Aupick, who had reached forty at the time of his marriage, who had put in six years campaigning for the Empire, and who bore up under a wound received in 1815 at the battle of Ligny, was a man of rigid piety and stiff morals. He was promoted to lieutenant colonel and assigned to Lyon during the latter part of 1830 to repress the uprisings there, together with Marshall Soult, Minister of War, and the Duke of Orléans. As soon as Charles and his mother joined him in the beginning of 1823, he placed the boy in a boarding school. Assuredly the Collège Royal Boarding School looked rather threatening, with its "gloomy structures, somber vaults, its bolted and grated entrances, and dank chapels with high walls which hid the sun," as Edgar Quinet, who had previously spent several years there, described it. The atmosphere of the town, with the coal fumes which Baudelaire still recalled thirty years later, was calamity itself at the time. The back streets of the Croix-Rousse rang frequently with rebellions, and the students themselves revolted in 1834. Beyond a doubt Charles took part in this. "After 1830, the college of Lyon, blows, battles with the professors and classmates, crushing fits of dejection."

Impressions follow upon each other briskly at this age however, and interesting pursuits were not lacking for this boy who possessed "a precocious love for beautiful works of literature," and who spent his recesses at school reciting passages from Hugo and Lamartine to his classmate, Hignard. His keen eyes were already aware of shapes and colors. The chapel that struck

Quinet only with its dampness left him with recollections of "variegated marbles" and of the "monstrous Jesuitical style" with which he was so taken in his later years.

It is unfortunate that the child should have been condemned unnecessarily to a bleak boarding-school life. One must realize, however, that the newly-appointed chief of the General Staff of the Seventh Military Division would have hardly had the time to supervise the schooling of his stepson, and that Baudelaire's mother perhaps would not have been capable of it. Furthermore, a semi-military discipline must have seemed most desirable for the son of a soldier who had himself been educated at La Flèche and Saint-Cyr. In any case, the young schoolboy does not manifest the least tendency toward melancholy in the one letter which we have from him from this period. He appears happy to take part in theatricals, and has only one cause for complaint: a sprain which keeps him from dancing. He has only one regret: the inadequacy of his achievements in school compared with those of his nephew, Théodore. "Tell him to make faces at me from down there!"

His stepfather, Colonel in 1834, Commander of the Legion of Honor in 1835, was appointed on January 9, 1836 Chief of the General Staff of the First Military Division stationed in Paris. Charles now became a boarder at the Lycée Louis-le-Grand, another somber building where, "under the square sky of loneliness," he came to know, as did many of the other boarders, "oppressive gloom," and the "torpor of cloistered lethargy." The crisis of puberty through which he was then passing was accentuated by his precocious sensuality and by his more or less Jansenist religious training which had developed a "mystic tendency" in him from childhood on. This turmoil was conditioned and aggravated by his reading of Chateaubriand and Sainte-Beuve: the Chateaubriand of *Les Natchez*, and the Sainte-Beuve of *Joseph Delorme* and *Volupté*.

His first literary preferences were so deeply rooted that he never repudiated them in later years. This explains his affectionate and respectful loyalty to Sainte-Beuve, though the latter—who to the last saw in him only a brilliant but somewhat dangerous disciple—never comprehended the power of his genius.

As in the tale of Amaury, the hero of *Volupté*, "in those days of pale adolescence," sensuality made his conscience vibrate and pivot between two extremes:

> Every mystic deep is within two steps of the abyss. . . .

These readings developed his taste for introspection without self-indulgence, though not wholly without smugness, and for

> The cruel art which a demon gave me at birth . . .
> Of drawing blood from a sore, and scratching my wounds.

At the same time, his modesty regarding his deeper feelings gave rise to provoking defense mechanisms; "mannerisms sometimes supercilious and sometimes shocking, arising from affectation," a "turbulent spirit, at times overflowing with mysticism, at times with an immorality and cynicism which knew no bounds." Such is the light in which he was seen by his teachers and classmates, but behind this sneering young face the profile of the aggressive dandy was already emerging.

It is likely that he had by that time dedicated himself to literature. He was "filled with enthusiasm for poetry, reciting passages from Hugo, Gautier, etc. at every turn." He began testing his own talent—a talent as yet quite uneven, and in which the influence of *Joseph Delorme* was dominant, but where genius blazed forth from time to time in the turn of a phrase:

> There water slumbers, night and day, in a sublime repose
> And never interrupts its *stormy silence*. . . .

and also—even this early—in the consciousness of Correspondences in the mystic sense of that word:

> One could say that the sky, in this solitude
> Studies itself in the water, and that those mountains there,
> Wrapped in solemn attention, are listening to
> A divine mystery which man does not hear.
>
> And when by chance a wandering cloud
> Shadows the silent lake in its passage,
> One thinks it the garment, or the transparent shadow,
> Of a travelling spirit floating in the skies.

These lines were inspired by a stay in the Pyrenees with Colonel Aupick around 1838, the dazzling memory of which he retained for a long time. He was to evoke this scenery and his serenity twenty years later in a prose poem, "Le Gâteau" (The Cake). If these journeys were so pleasant, certainly his companion could not have been distasteful to him. Later he complained about his "atrocious upbringing." But even then, when he was forty, he admitted that while fearing his stepfather he loved him, and he did not hesitate to add, "today I am wise enough to do him justice."

This friendly relationship was not weakened by a serious mishap which took place in his school career. Until that time he had substantially fulfilled the hopes his stepfather had placed in him. These are in evidence in Colonel Aupick's announcement to the headmaster: "I intend to present you with a gift, a pupil who will bring honor to your establishment." It is true that his behavior and dress were not up to the mark. His teachers reproached him for his flippancy, his character "somewhat out of the ordinary and at times bizarre." But they concurred in attributing to him "rather remarkable faculties . . . invention and finesse when he is so disposed." His poetic gifts found a means of expression in Latin exercises: he obtained first prize three years in a row, and a second prize in the national competition. However, on April 18, 1839, during his last year, the headmaster informed his family that the young Baudelaire had been expelled from school for having refused to "hand over a note that one of his friends had just slipped him." He tore up and swallowed the note, and declared "that he would accept any punishment rather than divulge his friend's secret." We may suppose that the Colonel easily forgave, and perhaps even commended, this scrupulous loyalty. Three months later, Charles, who was then preparing for his baccalaureate degree with a private tutor, stated that his "father" or "bosom friend," as he called his stepfather, "had always had a good feeling about him." On August 13, he announced his success at the examinations with affectionate cordiality, and at the same time congratulated his stepfather on his promotion to the rank of brigadier general. This promotion had just been announced that morning in the *Moniteur*.

Everything seemed to smile upon this young boy at the moment of his entrance into adult life. Hignard, his old friend from Lyon, found him "as good and as kind as in former times," and said that he had turned into not only "quite a good-looking young man," but one who was also "serious, studious, and religious." His stepfather, who in spite of his modest beginnings had attained a very high position, and had even established connections with the Duke of Orlèans, nourished "golden dreams of a promising future" for the boy. It was at this time that we find Baudelaire in the Bailly and Lévêque Student Home, 11 rue de l'Estrapade, close to the Law School, where he was registered periodically during 1839–1840, though it is unlikely that he ever attended courses.

Since the Bailly and Lévêque Home for Students disappeared long ago, biographers have reconstructed on the site, each according to his fancy, an Abbey of Thélème à la Rabelais, a kind of phalanstery, or a replica of the Vauquer Home of Balzac's *Père Goriot*. This "house of advanced study" had been founded some twenty years before by Bailly de Surcy, a former professor of philosophy at the Oratorians of Juilly. He was a deeply religious man, who had all his life been one of the most active supporters of the Catholic Church. His name appears on the list of founders and active members of most Catholic societies of his time; in particular he had organized—with his former student and spiritual son, Ozanam—the Society of Saint Vincent de Paul. The Society met under his own roof, and he still presided over it in Baudelaire's time. He had also founded the *Tribune Catholique*, which later became *L'Univers*. He directed the editing and printing of this publication, which took place in the buildings adjoining the Home. It is not surprising, therefore, that far from being a Rabelaisian Abbey of Thélème, the Home was "a *pension* where the well-born offspring of distinguished families, while enjoying moderate freedom, obtained along with bed and board the inestimable advantages of an inspiring and choice society where they could maintain the family customs with which they had been inculcated under the paternal roof."

It has never been formally established that Baudelaire actually was a boarder at the Home. But it was certainly one of his haunts, if only because his old schoolmate, Louis de la Gennevraye, roomed in the Home and was on the staff of

L'Univers. In his company, Baudelaire made friends with Le Vavasseur, Prarond, Dozon and Philippe de Chennevières. These young men who "toyed with the Muses" were not averse to mirth and folly. They did not, however, contest the established order of things. Most of them were Legitimists and militant Catholics. Baudelaire was no misfit in their society; his dress was notably fastidious, and already betrayed a tendency toward dandyism. One can picture him descending the staircase in the Bailly House, "slender, holding his head high, sporting an elongated waistcoat and impeccable cuffs, carrying a delicate cane topped by a tiny golden sphere, and stepping with a soft, slow, almost rhythmic cadence." His feelings were those of a "nice boy"; he wrote pious and sentimental verses containing much cautious advice. The sound of a hurdy gurdy reminded him of:

> My friend, whom I love so much
> Who told me once
> As we walked through the city
> What pleasure it gave him to hear a serenade
> During a period of dismal leisure . . .

For another, he recalled Sunday services in the country:

> This devotion of the fields, joyous and fresh
> Does it not recall for you, this sad and sweet memory
> The love that in other times you felt for Sundays?

On other occasions his thoughts were weightier:

> Alas! who has not cried out against others, against himself?
> Who has not said to God, "Forgive me, Lord,
> If no one loves me, if nothing has my heart.
> They have corrupted me; there is no one who loves You!"
>
> . . . .
>
> Then, ah, then we must surround ourselves with mystery
> Close ourselves off from view, and without arrogance, without rancor,
> Without saying to our neighbors, "I love only Heaven,"
> We must say to God, "Console my soul for the earth!"

One can thus sketch a most satisfactory picture of a perfect conformist who was the young Baudelaire. Needless to say, this portrait is inaccurate. No one was more conscious than he of the duality of human nature. But instead of giving way to it as did Verlaine—who tried to follow "simultaneously" the two paths along which he was carried—Baudelaire, who was too lucid to ever become so complacent, never ceased to be tortured by this conflict. One may be sure that he was already suffering from it at that time. These two stanzas sketch this early period "on a forgotten tablet."

> Great angel, who carry on your proud countenance
> The blackness of Hell, from which you have risen,
> Fierce and sweet subduer, who has placed me in a cage
> To serve as an example of your cruelty,
>
> Horror of my nights, Siren without breasts,
> Who drags me, always upright at my side,
> By my saintly robe or my sage's beard
> To offer me the poison of a shameless love . . .

One might even take the reference to a "sage's beard" literally, for Baudelaire sported a beard during his early adolescence. He was to reveal to Sainte-Beuve later on that he had known the temptations of "pernicious evenings" and "restless nights" from his boarding school days on:

> When the dark Venus, from the height of black balconies,
> Throws out the smell of musk from her bright censer.

It must be thoroughly understood that he saw in the foregoing rather the tauntings of the devil than the temptations of the flesh. On the other hand, he did not consider the weakness which kept him from resisting temptation as a personal failing. He felt that this weakness was native to man, but this did not diminish his sense of guilt. Going even further, he seems to have admitted very early that art itself, in requiring total knowledge of mankind, was inseparable from sin, and he chose with full commitment this "poet's existence" which he later charged his mother with not understanding. This is what Samuel Cramer, the hero of *La Fanfarlo* (1847) explains to Madame de Cosmelly: "We have set our hearts so completely on becoming worldly-wise, we have overstrained our microscopes to such an extent for the purpose of examining the ghastly protuberances and shameful blemishes with which we are covered and which we joyfully cultivate, that it is not possible for us to speak the language of common men. They live to live and we, alas, we live to understand."

On this issue Baudelaire parted company from his amiable associates of the Bailly Student Home. They gladly indulged in a few follies, always stopping in time, with literature serving merely as an outlet or diversion. But Baudelaire took poetry more seriously, and from this time on he broke with conformity and bourgeois conventions. To "evil unaware of itself" he preferred "conscious evil," confronting with some flamboyance his destiny as a sinner. These views appeared in a piece in which he already displayed a certain poetic flair and uncommon mastery, although as a whole the work was somewhat uneven. It has as its subject a certain Sarah, called Louchette, who is described in more or less unflattering terms. In this piece, it is obvious that Baudelaire overdoes some features in order to satisfy his taste for the picturesque, but he also painted human nature in all its wretchedness, and then set it against the powers of the spirit. He debases himself to her level:

> In order to have shoes, she sold her soul
> But the good God would laugh if, before this shame
> I played the hypocrite and pretended to be proud,
> I, who have sold my thoughts and wish to be known
> as an author.

At the end of the poem, she undergoes an apotheosis:

> Messieurs, do not despise the oaths, and the filth,
> On the painted mouth of this poor sinner
> Whom the goddess Hunger forced on a winter night
> To lift her petticoats in the open air.
>
> This bohemian girl is my all, my wealth
> My pearl, my jewel, my queen, my duchess
> She who has rocked me to sleep on her conquering bosom
> And with her two hands has rewarmed my heart.

Here is the human and moral significance of this supposedly degrading liaison. In another poem supposed to have been inspired by the same woman, which was later included in *Les Fleurs du Mal* (The Flowers of Evil), he showed, as in *La Fanfarlo*, the necessity of such experiences:

> The nobility of this evil in which you believe yourself wise,
> Has it never made you recoil in terror,
> When Nature, grand in her hidden schemes

Makes use of you, O woman, O queen of sin,
—Of you, vile animal—to mold a genius?

O filthy grandeur! sublime ignominy!

Such a conception of the life of a poet does not lack pitfalls. Baudelaire's worried friends wrote prodding warnings in rhyme, without realizing that he and they were no longer speaking the same language. As for the Aupick family, they were appalled, not so much by Charles' literary ambitions, as by his "indiscretions and undesirable connections." It was for the purpose of snatching him from "perdition in the streets of Paris," that the General and his wife decided to send him on a trip, not as punishment, certainly, but as a change. They did not force him into it, but they were eager to persuade him to go, and he let them have their way. Upon his departure, he wrote his parents a "nice letter" as a pledge of his loyal acquiescence.

Baudelaire embarked on June 9, 1841 at Bordeaux on the *Paquebot des mers du Sud,* due to sail as far as Calcutta under the captainship of Commander Saliz. The circumstances and the outcome of this cruise are well known, thanks to the long letter, actually a report, written by Saliz to General Aupick. He had not the least complaint to make regarding Baudelaire's manners, which had always been "mild and friendly" and who had been devoted to him. However, since he possessed more insight than the General, he foresaw after a few conversations "that it was too late to hope for a change of heart concerning Monsieur Beaudelaire's (sic) taste for literature as they understood it nowadays and his determination to forego any other occupation." Moreover, "his scathing opinions and declarations regarding all social relations" added to his solitude. This last point provides a confirmation of the connection which he had already perceived between the function of a poet and social nonconformity. Such an attitude rendered all contact with the other passengers impossible. This being, so eager for human understanding, who had never been able to live alone, and who could not do without an exchange of ideas, without someone to whom he could confide his thoughts and feelings, suffered profoundly from this self-imposed withdrawal. A violent storm "a phenomenon such as I have never witnessed in my long experience of sailing," as the captain stated, left him impassive. His disgust with this purposeless cruise, which he had undertaken with indifference, led him to refuse to continue further when the boat put in at Mauritius Island. After a stay of twenty days there, he consented to accompany Commander Saliz to Reunion Island for a stopover of forty-five days, upon the latter's promise to send him home. There—in spite of a local tradition concerning an idyllic love affair, and in spite of the inspiring scenery which was to color many of his later poems—his homesickness was so acute that his health was endangered.

For a long time there has been a doubt whether his references to Ceylon and Calcutta were pure fantasy. Some are found in his private notes and even in a letter to Ancelle, who could hardly be ignorant of the truth. However, a recent inquiry seems to have irrefutably demonstrated that he did not travel farther than Mauritius. One wonders whether he had not succeeded in persuading himself that he had reached India.

What is certain is that preparations to welcome him as a prodigal son were made, though not without misgivings. But his family could no longer ignore the facts: his determination had not been shaken, and the incompatibility of feeling between him and his stepfather rendered his presence at home extremely trying. It seems unlikely that there was at any given moment a violent break between them, but Baudelaire, hurt by the General's inflexibility and his reproaches, severed all connections with him. Circumstances were in his favor, as he had attained his majority on April 9, 1842 and had taken possession of his paternal inheritance. This consisted of property in Neuilly, for which he was to find takers at 75,000 francs the following year. Had he been able to wait as long as his brother Alphonse did, he could have obtained a much higher price for it. But he insisted upon his independence, not only because of his quarrel with his stepfather, but also because he had always put an extremely high price on liberty. It seemed to him that, on a moral plane, it represented an essential quality of man's existence, and that, even on a material plane, it was indispensable for the complete realization of his destiny.

2 · *The Norman School*

BAUDELAIRE brought back only two or three poems from his voyage, plus rough outlines or ideas for a few others. The sonnet "A une Dame créole" (To a Creole Lady) was sent from Reunion Island to the woman who inspired it—or rather, to her husband, for in curious contrast to his intellectual and social nonconformity, his customary refinement of behavior made it seem "proper, decent, and fitting that verses addressed to a lady by a young man should pass through the hands of her husband before she sees them." "A une Malabaraise" (To a Malabar Girl), which was published in 1846, must also have been written on Reunion Island, as was perhaps the case with "Bien loin d'ici" (Ever So Far from Here), which was not published until 1864, probably after extensive alterations.

The first two of these poems enable us to examine Baudelaire's very early style. This is particularly true of the sonnet which appears in the letter of October 20, 1841, and which is the oldest piece preserved for us in its original form. This poem does not as yet indicate absolute deftness or fullness of style. But the poetic and musical power of the words, their association or contrast, the alliteration and rhythm, are astonishing and combine to produce a tonality which is already quite Baudelairean in effect. All three poems, however, were outgrowths of incidental or exterior events, a kind of verse which Baudelaire was soon to abandon.

As for "L'Albatros" (The Albatross), tradition attributes to it approximately the same date of composition. It is supposed to "have been suggested by a happening during the crossing." According to Prarond, Baudelaire recited it "directly after his return." This statement has been challenged, though without decisive evidence. We know that the third stanza was added on Asselineau's suggestion in 1859, but it does seem likely that the others were written between 1841 and 1842.

Recollections of this voyage can be found in several other poems in *Les Fleurs du Mal,* namely in "La Vie antérieure" (A Former Life), "L'Homme et la mer" (Man and the Sea), "Parfum exotique" (Exotic Perfume), "La Chevelure" (Her Hair), and in several lines of "Moesta et errabunda" (Sad and Restless) and of "Le Voyage" (The Voyage). It also appears in several of the *Petits Poëmes en prose* (Little Poems in Prose): in "Un Hémisphère dans une chevelure" (A Hemisphere in a Head of Hair), and "La belle Dorothée" (The Beautiful Dorothy), among others.

It is now time to look into Baudelaire's literary activities at the time that he returned to the city and to the friendships which were so dear to him. Before his departure, he had already become associated with several writers outside of the Bailly Student Home: Édouard Ourliac, Gérard de Nerval, Balzac and Delatouche. These were his "first literary connections," according to his "Note autobiographique" (Autobiographical Note). It is interesting to read of his meeting with Balzac, as he related it to Le Vavasseur the following day: "Balzac and Baudelaire were walking in opposite directions on one of the quais of the Left Bank. Baudelaire stopped in front of Balzac and began laughing as if he had known him for ten years. Balzac stopped in his turn and replied with a resounding laugh, as if he had found a long-lost friend. And after having *recognized* each other at a glance and with a greeting, there they were, walking and talking in mutual rapture, incapable of astonishing each other." There is such lofty grandeur in this reciprocal outburst of joy following the intuitive perception of genius, that one can only hope that the story is perfectly accurate. Such true sympathy could not long exist between two people as different as they, and several years later Baudelaire remarked with biting severity on one of the indiscretions which Balzac was constantly committing without even realizing it. This one was in *Comment on paie ses dettes quand on a du génie* (How to Pay One's Debts when one is endowed with genius), 1845. But, as he wrote once of Sainte-Beuve and Delacroix, "the affections arise mostly from the mind," and the truly sublime heights of Balzac's thought, its supreme strength, always inspired him with the greatest and most sincere admiration. There even existed a genuine intellectual bond between them. Though Baudelaire himself did not embrace Swedenborgianism as a religion, as Balzac did, he nonetheless displayed interest in the works and ideas of the Swedish mystic, and the two Frenchmen met more than once on this ground.

It is worthy of note that all the names mentioned by Baudelaire in his "Note autobiographique" were those of writers who were more or less involved in speculations of a spiritual nature. The brilliant chronicler, Édouard Ourliac, who had occasionally collaborated with Balzac, became a convert at that time and probably made Baudelaire's acquaintance in the offices of *L'Univers*. Baudelaire had praised Ourliac's talent more than once, though he also abused him occasionally. He proposed to write an article about him as a contribution to a newspaper which was planned to appear in 1851 or 1852 under the title *Le Hibou philosophe*. That the works of Nerval are imbued with mysticism and Illuminism is well known, and even Delatouche seems to have been initiated by a disciple of Saint-Martin. In any case, Baudelaire was familiar in varying degrees with such acquaintances.

The tale of Baudelaire's leave-taking of Balzac prior to his departure for Mauritius Island—a leave-taking at which Gérard de Nerval and Delatouche are supposed to have been present—has been told in detail. There is not a word of truth in this story: at that time Delatouche was at odds with Balzac, who had just fiercely attacked him in his *Revue parisienne*. As for the unfortunate Gérard de Nerval, his reason had already begun to fail him, and from February until November of 1841 he was continuously confined to an insane asylum.

It was actually only after his return that Baudelaire really began a literary life and cut all ties with his bourgeois upbringing. He had met Gérard de Nerval through Ourliac; the latter had also introduced him to Victor Hugo and Pétrus Borel. The juxtaposition of these last two names may seem strange, but the fact remains that each of these writers, in his own way, held an important place in Baudelaire's thought. The enthusiastic letter from Baudelaire to Sainte-Beuve, from which we have previously quoted, probably marked the beginning of their acquaintance at this period. He also met Alphonse Esquiros, who may have drawn his attention to social problems from this time on—a simple hypothesis, though a likely one. Lastly, Baudelaire met Théophile Gautier, whom he had already viewed from a distance and without much cordiality for some time—as a few rather harsh allusions made in 1845 and 1846 indicate. In spite of his sincere admiration for Gautier, Baudelaire always maintained some reservations about him: they are still apparent in 1863, in a passage of "L'Oeuvre et la vie d'Eugène Delacroix" (The Life and Work of Eugene Delacroix), which came some time after the glowing dedication of *Fleurs du Mal* and the lofty "Notice" of 1859.

These assorted individuals could not have been counted among Baudelaire's friends at that time—Sainte-Beuve and Gautier alone were to become his friends later on. His real associates were still those from the days of the Bailly Student Home. Several of them, like him, had poetic ambitions and some hope of getting into print. Like any group of young writers, they were in need of a standard, or in more modest terms, a label. They adopted the hardly incriminating title of "The Norman School." This geographic designation probably came about through Le Vavasseur, one of the few Normans of the group. He was the animating spirit behind the group, and the one of them who was closest to Baudelaire. They dispensed with both plans and manifestoes. These young men, who were passionately devoted to poetry and seeking their own way, were without metaphysical or material anxieties: they were well-born and blessed with private means.

Baudelaire easily fitted into this merry gang. "Ah!" exclaimed Jules Buisson, "I warrant that all of us, the Norman School and Baudelaire alike, found life worth living in 1843, when we used to dine at the Tour d'Argent, on the Ile Saint-Louis, or anywhere else that we wished." This somewhat superficial and occasionally spiteful contemporary was mistaken in not making the slightest distinction between Baudelaire and his company. However, we should keep in mind that the Baudelaire of that period did not as yet wear the mask of anxiety and bitterness which the photographs of Nadar, Carjat and Neyt, as well as the portraits of Courbet, Manet and Bracquemond later revealed. In order to picture him during this period of comparative happiness, we must refer to the portrait painted by his friend, Deroy. Deroy was a promising painter who met with an untimely death at twenty-three, but he will be remembered for this portrait which hangs in Versailles. In it, Baudelaire's gaze is already marked by that attentive steadiness, a bit troubled and troubling, with which we are familiar. But his mouth is relaxed and slightly smiling, very gentle, with only a touch of irony. His stance is unstudied, with his body leaning toward the left and resting on one elbow. The feature which transforms him is, in Asselineau's words, "a youthful, fine, rich beard, somewhat curly in the region of the chin and the cheeks." The prevailing impression is one of delicacy and unqualified distinction. His dress shows a certain refinement and elegance: "The waistcoat, about which he must have thought at some length, is exaggerated into a funnel shape crowned by his head, and tapers into minute coattails in the back; the narrow trousers are anchored by foot-straps stretched over impeccably polished boots. The shirt collar is wide, with matching cuffs of fine white linen." This recalls Nadar's description of him, sporting "pale pink" gloves and an "ox-blood" necktie, the only color accents in an otherwise black and white composition. He was occasionally fond of slipping "a blue wagoner's smock, nice and crisp, with brand new pleats" over his black outfit. He rarely wore a hat.

He was to take great care with his appearance all his life. But during his youth his outward and inward qualities combined so that meeting him was a striking visual and intellectual experience. It left Banville dazzled. "If ever a human being could be called attractive, it would be he. He possessed at once distinction, pride, and elegance, a beauty both boyish and manly, the charm of a cadenced and well-pitched voice, and a most winning speech, which expressed his whole nature. His eyes, overflowing with life and thought, spoke in unison with his full but finely-drawn and red lips, while an indefinable vibration trembled along his long, dense and silky black hair. In him I saw what I had never seen before: a man as I had thought men should be, in his dauntless springtime glory, and upon hearing him address me with fond good will, I felt the turbulence which one feels in the presence of genius."

Though not an adherent of the Norman School, Banville caused real enthusiasm among its members when he published his *Cariatides* (Caryatids) in 1842. "I remember," Baudelaire was to write subsequently, "that we leafed through this volume in astonishment, where we found so many jumbled treasures heaped in a disorderly pile." In fiery admiration, he dedicated a vibrant sonnet to the young poet. This sonnet found its way into the posthumous edition of *Fleurs du Mal*, although it was certainly not written for that volume. Banville himself prepared this posthumous edition, with the help of Asselineau.

> You have laid hold of the Goddess by the hair
> And with such a grip, that one takes you
> (Seeing your air of ease, your beautiful nonchalance)
> For a young hoodlum flinging his girl to the ground . . .

Banville was quite young—he had not yet reached twenty—and his work was a splendid illustration of a tendency common to the literary taste of the young at that time: the cult of form, or, to use the familiar catchword, of Art for Art's Sake. This aesthetic doctrine, which originated in German philosophy, was recorded by Benjamin Constant in his *Journal* as early as 1804, and was heralded by Madame de Staël in her book, *De l'Allemagne*. It began gradually to gather followers, thanks to the courses given by Victor Cousin and Jouffroy, and perhaps also to the statements of Heinrich Heine, who descended on Paris in 1831. Its essence could already be found in the prefaces of Gautier in 1832 *(Albertus)* and in 1835 *(Mademoiselle de Maupin)*. From 1834 on, people began talking about a "School" of Art for Art's Sake. Well before the Parnassian movement, the groupings emerged. Baudelaire himself bore witness to this "School" in his notes for the *Hibou philosophe*. Among the various literary schools which he took upon himself to attack was the *École plastique* (Plastic School) of Theophile Gautier.

He differentiated between it and the *École païenne* (Pagan School), which went back to Banville, and against which Baudelaire later wrote the well-known article in the *Semaine théâtrale* of January 22, 1852.

The differences seem to have been more personal than doctrinal in nature. Banville added nothing new to Gautier's ideas. The latter bore the responsibility for both schools of thought, which, in fact, later merged to form the Parnassian School. On several occasions Gautier formulated a theory of poetry which could be reduced to the exclusive cult of formal, and consequently plastic, beauty. "Flee always the musical epithet for the epithet that paints," he said to his friends. Indeed, he soon chose contour rather than color: "It has been said that painting is the sister art of poetry, but this is truer of sculpture. . . . Color can minimize the shortcomings of the prose writer and the painter, but in poetry and in sculpture the style is indispensable, and every element must be perfect." This is how he stated his position in 1841, and one can be sure that this article, which appeared in the *Revue des Deux Mondes,* did not escape the attention of the inhabitants of the Bailly Student Home.

This was not the line of thought adopted by the first generation of Romantics. "Romanticism," stated Jouffroy in 1826, in the course of his lectures on aesthetics, "tends to spiritualize material nature." Poetry was then seeking musical, rather than descriptive expression, and often boasted of owing more to inspiration than to "art," in the limited sense of that word. The Norman School did not positively stand behind the new doctrine, but it did acknowledge the prestige of form. "Gustave Le Vavasseur," Baudelaire was to write, "has always been passionately found of master-strokes. For him a difficulty has all the seductions of a nymph. He delights in obstacles; epigrams and puns intoxicate him; there is no music more pleasing to his ears than that of triple, quadruple, and multiple rhymes."

Baudelaire no doubt found himself violently opposed to Gautier on many points. "Spirituality is not for me," declared d'Albert, the hero of *Mademoiselle de Maupin,* who "willingly does without a soul or mind." There was no possible agreement between the two on this point. Baudelaire's thinking was always steeped in spirituality, even when his faith failed:

> Every mystic deep is just two steps from doubt. . . .

The line quoted above is from the letter to Sainte-Beuve which was probably written during this period, that is to say around 1842 or 1843. Nevertheless, Baudelaire was too much the artist to be able to remain aloof from the concept of beauty for its own sake. He was probably tempted by this idea when he wrote his sonnet "La Beauté" (Beauty):

> I am beautiful, O mortals, as a dream in stone . . .

This poem can itself be taken as a magnificent example of the *École plastique*. But we would make a serious mistake if we found the artistic credo of the poet in this sonnet. It was a vision, a momentary and pleasing dream; but this beauty was not his own, and it is not sure that he ever embraced it. A poem of the same period, "Allégorie" (Allegory), was based on the same aesthetic; nevertheless, Baudelaire was to place it in that chapter of *Les Fleurs du Mal* which dealt with criminal offenses.

Gautier prided himself on being the first to reawaken an interest in Antiquity. He boasted about it to the Goncourt brothers. "When I sang the praises of Antiquity in the preface to *Mademoiselle de Maupin*, it heralded a new beginning." After the publication of *Les Cariatides*, Banville followed in his footsteps. But Gautier was less of an innovator than he thought. From the very beginning, the sap of Antiquity had coursed through Romantic poetry. Gautier himself conceded that "modern poetry begins with André Chénier." But now the concern was not with classical Antiquity, nor with that of the painter, Louis David. Artistic expression was rejuvenated due to a more precise understanding of Greek aesthetic, brought to life by the Elgin marbles—which were on view in London from 1816 on—and by the Venus de Milo, which could be seen in the Louvre in 1821. Themes inspired by Antiquity were common to Vigny and Musset, as well as to Alphonse Rabbe and Maurice de Guérin. It is true that in the latter writers, as in Ballanche, Edgar Quinet and Victor de Laprade, Antiquity was accompanied by a confused religious mysticism, and it is hard to know how much to ascribe to verbalism, how much to allegory, and how much to faith. Ballanche and Laprade linked Antiquity to Christianity, while Gautier and Banville paid homage to a formal Beauty, and Louis Ménard constructed a mystic paganism in which Christ was admitted to the ranks of the other divinities:

> The ideal temple to which my prayers ascend
> Encompasses all the Gods that the world has known.

Baudelaire's precise and highly ordered thinking inevitably rejected such rubbish and pseudo-religiosity. However, before embracing the beauty of man and the modern world in all its tragic grandeur, he couldn't help casting a backward glance of regret upon this more or less imaginary Antiquity, where wholesomeness, harmony, strength and beauty reigned:

> I love the memory of those naked ages . . .

This poem echoes Laprade and Musset, and possibly Mathurin Régnier also, who at that time had already written in his fifth *Satire*:

> Fathers from aged centuries, exemplars of life . . .
> In the days of yore, virtue, simple and pure,
> Without guile or fiction, imitated nature. . . .

This poet was certainly known to the Norman School. But before we deal with Régnier, let us conclude our discussion of Gautier's influence on Baudelaire. This influence is much less apparent in aesthetic theory than it is in actual practice. Above all, Baudelaire admired Gautier's matchless technique: he was a verbal virtuoso and a skillful poet. Throughout his life this admiration did not flag, though it did not increase in intensity. For him, Théophile Gautier was the creator of *Albertus, La Comédie de la Mort* (The Comedy of Death), and *España* (Spain). It was to this person that he dedicated *Les Fleurs du Mal,* and not to the author of *Emaux et Camées* (Enamels and Cameos). This last-mentioned collection of poems had appeared five years before, even in the "Notice" of 1859, but Baudelaire hardly mentioned it. He was attracted instead by the Gautier who, as he stated in the "Notice," "has, on his part, kept alive the great school of melancholy created by Chateaubriand," the romantic—and to some extent even spiritual—Gautier.

That he was not taken in by the appeal of Art for Art's Sake was proven by the fact that he was able to divide his admiration between Théophile Gautier and Sainte-Beuve: two totally different human and literary types, who, needless to say, hardly displayed much sympathy for each other. Both through his poetry and through *Volupté,* Sainte-Beuve exercised an influence over the youth of that time which we are now inclined to ignore too easily, just as we ignore the works themselves. The Norman School, however, gave Sainte-Beuve his due. Le Vavasseur published his first poems under the pseudonym of G. Delorme. Prarond entitled his first collection of verses *Impressions et pensées d'Albert* (Impressions and Thoughts of Albert), in imitation of *Poésies et pensées de Joseph Delorme* (Poems and Thoughts of Joseph Delorme), by Sainte-Beuve. As for Baudelaire, he throve on both Sainte-Beuve's poetry and his novel. Concerning *Volupté,* he wrote:

> I absorbed all of it: the vapors, the perfumes,
> The sweet whispering of dead memories,
> The long entwining of symbolic phrases,
> Murmuring rosaries of mystic madrigals:
> —A voluptuous book, if ever one was written!

Ending his epistle to Sainte-Beuve on an almost passionate note, he said:

> For, face to face with you, I am like a lover
> Face to face with a ghost, whose gestures are full of cunning
> Whose hand and eye both have unspeakable charms
> To draw out my life force. All beings that one loves
> Are cups of acid to be drunk, eyes shut;
> And the heart, pierced through, drawn on by sorrow,
> Dies daily, blessing the arrow.

From time to time, Baudelaire extended subtle compliments to Sainte-Beuve, concerning both his prose style and his achievements as a critic. But it was mainly the poetry which captivated him, for he found in it that aura of intimacy and confiding whispers which was also so characteristic of his own nature. "The first," Jules Laforgue was to note, "who spoke in the quiet tones of confession, and did not pretend to be inspired." Though he was referring to Baudelaire, was not Sainte-Beuve in fact the first? Does not Joseph Delorme's tormented soul bear some similarity to Baudelaire's? Which of the two provides us with an unimaginable confusion "overflowing with grotesque fantasies, recent remembrances, lofty schemes turned to naught, judicious forethoughts followed by outrageous deeds, surges of piety coming upon the heels of blasphemous acts which ferment and stir about in fathoms of despair"? No, this is not Baudelaire's legacy to us, though these lines, which are taken, in fact, from the *Vie de Joseph Delorme* (Life of Joseph Delorme), could easily mislead us. Baudelaire's own appraisal of Sainte-Beuve was entirely unvarnished. He was perfectly aware of the latter's shortcomings, which he bravely communicated to him in a letter in 1866. Leaving aside the question of genius, *Joseph Delorme* could simply be called "The Flowers of Evil in the bud." Baudelaire himself pointed this out to Sainte-Beuve, and one can only regret that his plans for an article on "Sainte-Beuve ou Joseph Delorme jugé par l'auteur des *Fleurs du Mal*" (Sainte-Beuve or Joseph Delorme Judged by the Author of *The Flowers of Evil*) never materialized. Aside from certain overall similarities (which we should certainly not overestimate), several poems of this period can be directly traced to the influence of *Joseph Delorme*, though they were even then superior to this work. We may cite, among others, "Le Soleil" (The Sun), as well as two pieces which grew out of personal situations: "Je n'ai pas oublié, voisine de la ville . . ." (I have never forgotten, close to the town . . .), and "La servante au grand coeur dont vous étiez jalouse . . ." (The noble-hearted servant, of whom you were jealous . . .).

Baudelaire also inherited from Sainte-Beuve and Gautier a predilection for the Pléiade, for Mathurin Régnier, and for the libertine poets of the reign of Louis XIII. He and his circle throve on the work of that period, and they took pleasure in recalling, as did Prarond in his sonnet,

> The ancient style of the ancient Scarron.

On other occasions their verses bordered on pastiche, as does Baudelaire's "A une mendiante rousse" (To a Red-Haired Beggar Girl), which follows a rhythm devised by Ronsard (who is mentioned by name along with Belleau), and which even employed archaic words and spellings in its original form. He valued the vigor and dash of the (as yet unconstrained) poetic language of that time, and made a close study of it. In Banville's first remarks to Asselineau concerning Baudelaire, he spoke of him as "a highly exceptional poet *who was much acquainted with and influenced by Régnier*," while another friend of the epoch, Charles Cousin, described him as "groping his way between Villon and Ronsard, fascinated both by contemporary art and by the sonnets of bygone times."

This picturesque and highly colorful poetry can be linked with the work of Baudelaire's immediate predecessors, the Jeune-France—a work which was fervently perused by Baudelaire's generation. Jeune-France is a loose and ill-fitting term for this group which could in fact be called the second generation of Romantics (in which case Baudelaire and his contemporaries formed the third generation). The Jeune-France—these youthful combattants who had fought the battle of *Hernani*—were, in spite of their unanimous adulation for their elders, and for Victor Hugo in particular, different from the preceding generation in every respect. Lamartine, Vigny, and Hugo had belonged to the royal or imperial aristocracy. They were admitted to the most select society, were subsidized and honored by the monarchy, and functioned almost as poets laureate. Although they all affected melancholy poses on lake shores, they were married and in good circumstances for the most part. At times their works were violently condemned, but they were also vibrantly applauded. Their "mal du siècle" was basically ornamental: it shared no ties with the "mal du siècle" of an Obermann or a René. When Chateaubriand wrote *Les Natchez*, he was forlorn, unknown, and nearly destitute; Sénancour injected into his works all the hopelessness of an aborted future, and the dismal fury which drove Byron across Europe was the expression of a tormented life.

This last mentioned Romanticism—the Romanticism of Chateaubriand, and of Byron—was the kind which was shared by the Jeune-France, only with more bitterness and, let us admit, less grandeur. Pétrus Borel, Lassailly, Théophile Dondey (Philothée O'Neddy), and their like, were deprived of both fortune and connections. Want, sickness, insanity, and suicide took merciless tolls in their midst. Some just succumbed to misery, as did Hégésippe Moreau and a few others. But here is a group of rebels whose uneven efforts startle us with honest and poignant accusations. They were not people sated with self-satisfaction. They were members of a generation that had pinned its hopes on the Revolution of 1830, and they were deeply disenchanted to see the results of the Revolution nullified by a grasping and ruthless bourgeoisie. They were Republican, in their own fashion, though not in the usual sense of the word. "Lycanthropy, that's my kind of Republicanism!" Pétrus Borel cried out in the Preface of *Rapsodies* (Rhapsodies) in 1832: "If I speak of a Republic, it is because the word implies the greatest possible liberty that civilization can allow. I am a Republican because I can't be a savage." And the following year, in the Foreword of *Feu et Flamme* (Fire and Flame), Philothée O'Neddy emphasized that his thinking was based on absolute scorn of "the social, and above all, the political, structure." Both their prose and their verse were aggressive and assaulted the reader with excesses and liberties. They gloried in gruesome topics and settings:

> Behold the words that a young skeleton
> Uttered with crossed arms, erect in his shroud,
> Well before crimson dawn
> In the populous cemetery where I wandered forlorn . . .

In his novel entitled *Trialph,* Lassailly comes close to self-parody in his depiction of atrocities. In one of the *Contes immoraux* (Immoral Tales) of Pétrus Borel, which was later to inspire Baudelaire with an idea for a play, the schoolboy Passereau makes a statement to his executioner, "I fervently desire that you guillotine me!" In 1839, Pétrus Borel finally published his masterpiece, *Madame Putiphar,* a work appreciated by Baudelaire for "its genuine epic quality in several scenes." Baudelaire also remarked on "the strange, intense poem with its ringing sonority and almost primitive savor," which served as a prologue to the novel.

Baudelaire was to write subsequently that: "Romanticism would have been incomplete without Pétrus Borel," and it is possible to detect in the variegated music of *Les Fleurs du Mal* a note which echoes his harsh but strident tones. The members of the Norman School delighted in extravagances such as these. They all partook of them heartily, especially Prarond, who made ample use of skeletons and tombs:

In its tearless orb my eye had gone astray,
Worms gnawed at my skull as on an empty nutshell . . .

But this gruesome paraphernalia, which remained superficial in the work of Prarond, and which simply cancelled itself out by its own excess in many of the works of the Jeune-France, took on a deeper significance in Baudelaire's poems. These effects corresponded to Baudelaire's true feelings and they were charged with spirituality. At times they were no more than aesthetic fantasies, as in "La Géante" (The Giantess). But poems like "L'Ame du vin" (The Soul of Wine), "Le Vin des chiffonniers" (The Ragpickers' Wine), "Le Crépuscule du matin" (Morning Twilight), "Les deux bonnes Soeurs" (The Two Good Sisters), "La Rebelle" (The Rebel), and, above all, "Une Charogne" (A Carrion) gave evidence even then of Baudelaire's perfect mastery of the poetic vehicle. The richness of the inner life of this poet placed him on a different footing than the common run of the more or less weak writers discussed above.

This was not a period of revolt for him. Though Baudelaire willingly gave up the bourgeois comforts that the first generation of Romanticists had found necessary, his circumstances remained good at that time, and he was, in fact, the envy of more than a few of his friends. Not subject to material cares, he had, in 1843, "found royal quarters in a historic residence, the famous Hotel Pimodan, which several notables of the artistic and literary worlds had sanctified by their stay." (We quote from Asselineau.) He gave no thought to money, spending it carelessly on trifles, paintings, and art objects. It would scarcely have been appropriate or sincere if he had set himself up as a victim while youth and genius seemed to allow him unlimited means. His choice of imagery was not governed by revolt, but simply by aggressive brazenness. In their original versions both "L'Ame du vin" and "Le Vin des chiffoniers" ended on notes of gratitude to God. Even in "Le Rebelle" he contrasted to the callous sinner the boundless patience and charity of his good Angel, and it would be erroneous to believe that the author took sides with the sinner. The penetrating quality of these verses can be ascribed to the poetic intensity which Baudelaire attained in them in his representation of the human condition.

The indisputable superiority of these poems, when viewed

beside the well-bred fantasies of a Le Vavasseur or a Prarond, was not as yet obvious to most readers, though some of them do seem to have sensed the difference. They had decided to collect the poems of four of them, including Auguste Dozon, whose pen-name was Argonne, in a volume of poems entitled *Vers* (Verse), which appeared in 1843. Actually however, only three of them collaborated. Le Vavasseur later related how, upon receiving Baudelaire's contribution, he had permitted himself to make a few observations: "I had hoped, thoughtless and imprudent friend that I was, to improve upon the poet. Baudelaire said nothing, did not lose his temper, and withdrew his collaboration. He was right. He was made of a higher grade of stuff than our homespun calico and we went into print without him." However, Poulet-Malassis, Arsène Houssaye and Jules Levallois have attributed to Baudelaire—who was none too eager to publish verses under his own name—one or two pieces signed by Privat d'Anglemont, a striking bohemian figure who was quite unscrupulous about accepting the credit for creations coming from strange pens when he himself was short of inspiration. Some people have inferred as a result that Baudelaire, either through his propensity for hoaxes, or through innate shyness, may have published in the same manner on other occasions. Monsieur Jules Mouquet, a learned scholar endowed with a rather daring imagination, compiled a volume of *Vers retrouvés* (Newly-found Poems), comprising thirty-four pieces formerly attributed to Prarond or Privat d'Anglemont in *Vers*. His "discovery" stirred up much controversy without producing any definite conclusions. No doubt Monsieur Mouquet's theory is an extreme one, but one can not exclude the possibility that there are among the poems of Prarond a few misplaced verses by Baudelaire. The most plausible conclusion is that they both shared—for a while at least—a community of inspiration, and that both had slaked their thirst in common waters.

The fact which prompted Monsieur Mouquet to formulate his dubious theory was that he had actually uncovered evidence of a collaboration between Baudelaire and Prarond, or, more exactly, of a "planned collaboration" (to use the words of Prarond himself). The work in question remained unfinished and was finally abandoned. In later years, neither of the authors ever referred to this caprice of their younger days, to which they apparently ascribed no importance. It is, indeed, not an easily classifiable work: tragedy, comedy, or farce? One hesitates in reading the piece, whose cast of characters includes *Idéolus*—from whom the play takes its title—Socrates, Nobilis, Nubilis, and Forniquette. A later manuscript leads one to suspect that Prarond had at some time hoped to salvage the play and had tried to give it a bit more credibility by giving the cast Spanish names and changing the title to *Manoël*.

Its verse is both striking and vivid, though it is seldom poetic. At times it borders on a parody of Romantic drama. Nevertheless, *Idéolus* is not totally lacking in interest. Its theme is directly related to the fundamental currents of Baudelaire's thought: the problem of the inherent duality of man's nature—the continual conflict caused by his yearning for the ideal in a world of corporal needs. The cynical Socrates is set against Ideolus the sculptor, smitten with the ideal. Moreover, as in *Les Fleurs du Mal*, and especially in the poems of 1857, this struggle is imbedded in the soul of the poet himself and is the one cause of his inability to bring the work to the conclusion which he had originally conceived for it:

To hear always in oneself the inner battle,
Two men who fight without rest, to steal the time from each other

. . .

On the one hand, disgust, long weariness,
The impotence which makes one lose heart,
On the other hand, that voice which moves one's bowels
And shakes, from time to time, the very walls. . . .

Thus, if we look carefully, we can already discern, during the glorious days of the Norman School, a portrait of the real Baudelaire: but the colors are still faint, the outlines blurred, and the shadows barely visible.

3 · *A Sinister Storm*

IN ALL PROBABILITY, it was towards the end of 1842 that Baudelaire made the acquaintance of the mulatto woman who went by the name of Jeanne Duval or Lemer, but whose true identity has never been unveiled. It seems that she had for some time been playing bit parts in the Théâtre de la Porte Saint Antoine. The part she played in Baudelaire's life is worth defining with some precision. Most biographers have not spared her, calling her ugly, unintelligent, unfaithful, and greedy, and regarding her as Baudelaire's bad angel, *la Vénus noire,* the cause of all his misfortunes. Banville and Nadar, however, who both knew her extremely well, found her beautiful and seductive, with mat rather than dark complexion, eyes "like saucers," a sumptuous head of hair, and a stately carriage. Nadar affirmed that she was proud and unselfish, and that she would accept "nothing under whatever form offered," not even a treat in a restaurant. Lastly, Baudelaire stated that "his peace of mind lay solely in her," and that she was "his sole diversion, his only pleasure, and unique friend." Could one imagine that a stupid and wretched creature, such as Jeanne Duval has been believed to be, would have been capable of playing such a role in Baudelaire's life? He never abandoned her, even when she was helpless and had long been separated from him. On his hospital bed in Brussels in 1866, he was still suffering—as his mother had to admit—on account of his inability to help her further. True, she had by then been asking him for assistance over a period of several years. But this improvident had relapsed into a state of near infancy, and she had no other recourse. No doubt he must have at some time promised her a small income, calculating rashly on the earnings from his writing. Of course, one could wish that Baudelaire had found a mate more worthy of him. But this is no reason for holding this hapless woman accountable for the poet's life. We underestimate Baudelaire's force of character if we imagine him to be a "virtuous young man" floundering in bad company: actually, he was the totally lucid master of his destiny.

We must concede, on all accounts, that the presence of this woman in Baudelaire's life was rather beneficial, at least in the beginning. The "cycle" dedicated to Jeanne Duval in *Les Fleurs du Mal* confirms this theory. In it, the three or four violent pieces, such as "Tu mettrais l'univers entier dans ta ruelle" (You'd take to bed the whole world), have been definitely proven by Prarond to take their inspiration from Sarah, the so-called Louchette, or to have their origins in obvious literary sources, as do "Le Vampire" (The Vampire), "Remords posthume" (The Remorse of the Dead), and "Duellum" (The Duel). These permit only the most dubious personal interpretation. The other poems in which we can unquestionably recognize the figure of the mulatto woman constitute the most fervent and heartfelt hymns of love. This is especially true of "Le Balcon" (The Balcony) and the four sonnets comprising "Un Fantôme" (An Apparition), an unforgettable farewell to a person not only loved, but fondly cherished.

In any case, though this liaison does not seem to have had the vicious or sinister character frequently ascribed to it, it nevertheless was certainly not instrumental in restoring the Aupicks' trust in Baudelaire. He was causing them increasing uneasiness over the expenses he incurred in his life as a dandy. These expenditures, though not exorbitant, were disproportionate to his modest income. His capital quickly melted, and his literary activities did not furnish any appreciable returns. These activities could very well have seemed trifling to his family, since until 1844 he had merely published a few anonymous articles. Anxious to preserve her son's financial security, Madame Aupick finally yielded to the advice of her family and friends, and requested the appointment of a legal guardian for her son. This motion was granted by the Tribunal on September 21, 1844.

There is no doubt that this measure was taken in Baudelaire's interest, and was logically justifiable. However, the disastrous results it had on his feelings and actions were not offset by the advantages his family had anticipated for him, and the private agreement which Baudelaire himself had suggested would certainly have been preferable. His reaction was extremely violent. He denied without any further ado the restrictions placed upon him. Instead of adjusting his life to its new circumstances, he refused to acknowledge them, except by the implacable fury and humiliation that he felt forever after. The event took on a deep significance for him: "Does it matter what it actually means to most people," he wrote to his mother, "if I take it in a totally different way? . . . So, fix one thing firmly in your mind which you seem to forget constantly; it is that, unhappily for me, in all truth I am not made like other men." These pronouncements were probably not taken with too much gravity by Baudelaire's family; yet we know today that they were no idle words. More than just pride or feelings were at stake: his entire spiritual life was jarred. "I emphatically spurn anything that undermines my liberty." He referred here to material liberty, but it is quite likely that for him it was closely linked with spiritual liberty, upon which his entire thinking was based.

Nothing was more foreign to him than the concept of predestination. Regardless of the depth of his religious feelings, his conscience always remained aware of responsibility—that is to say, of human liberty. At that time, he had already made a choice which involved his whole future. He had deliberately broken with a society whose commands and conventions he rejected. The judicial decree of September 21 caught him by the collar and dragged him back, a subject of that same society. Understandably, his entire being revolted from the injustice done to him. Even fifteen years later, the decree of guardianship remained in his eyes "that appalling evil that destroyed my life, darkened all my days, and cast over all my thoughts a hue of hate and despair."

He was even more deeply affected than he would admit to others and, perhaps, even to himself. In spite of the confidence which he felt in himself and in his future, and which some of his letters to his mother reveal, he was too much of a realist to deceive himself about the extent of either his successes or his misconduct. But these material and spiritual failings, which could have been remedied with time, had now received their official consecration. Baudelaire felt himself immured in his failure and in his personal guilt: therein lay the gravest and bitterest consequence of the decision, which had been made against his will, and with which he refused to comply. It was harmful to him in exact proportion to his insubordination.

The small monthly allowance issued to him by the lawyer Ancelle who served as his guardian would have provided him with a modest living, if he had made the proper adjustments. But even if he had wished to do so, it would not have been easy for him, used as he was to his life of luxury. He was hardly capable of resisting his love of beautiful things, of furniture, pictures, and curios. After a few months which he passed in the throes of despair, he abandoned the struggle and made an attempt to end his life by stabbing himself with a knife on June 30, 1845.

Legend has dismissed this suicide attempt as counterfeit for quite some time. We are told that the knife thrust was "intended to pierce someone else's heart," meaning that of his mother. But the letter and will addressed to Ancelle, which have finally been published in their entirety, no longer leave us room to question Baudelaire's intention at the time. We must believe that the attempt was sincere, not only because of the tone of the letter, but even more so bcause of the line of its reasoning. Far from indicting the decree of guardianship, which he does not even mention, the letter tends to vindicate it. Baudelaire explains his action as a sentence of execution which he pronounced on himself: "I am taking my life because I am of no use to others—and dangerous to myself." Bequeathing all his possessions to Jeanne Duval, he beseeches Ancelle to watch over her and advise her: "Show her my hideous example—how a disorderly life and mind lead to somber despair or to total annihilation." He was not impelled by the pressure of his obligations: "My debts have never caused me grief. Nothing is easier for me than to rise above things like that."

To all appearances, it was the court decision which brought him to this depth of despondency, but only in that it forced him to the realization of his failure. This episode marked the end of his youth, of those "sunlit days" which he described in *La Fanfarlo*, "when morning never greeted us with knees benumbed or wearied by the effort of dreaming, when our unclouded eyes laughed back at all of nature, when our souls were alive and thought only of pleasure, when we heaved soundless sighs free of pride!" He was then only twenty-four years old. But his spiritual destiny, the only one that mattered to him, had already been resolved. His bodily wound was of no consequence, but the wound to his soul was never to heal again.

4 · *The* Corsaire-Satan

AS SOON AS SHE WAS NOTIFIED, his mother had him brought to her home, which was the Hôtel de la Place, located on the Place Vendôme and occupied by General Aupick in his capacity as Chief of the General Staff of the Paris Division. Baudelaire remained there for five or six months. But the moral and material advantages which he discovered under the family roof did not persuade him to make peace with his stepfather: "I find it impossible to become what your husband wishes me to be," he wrote to his mother, on notifying her of his departure, "hence it would amount to robbery to remain longer in his home. Lastly, I do not believe that it would be decent for me to be treated as he is apparently disposed to treat me." There was neither a quarrel nor a violent parting, only an incompatibility between the two personalities, and, furthermore, between two views of life. It is important to keep in mind that Baudelaire voluntarily gave up a comfortable existence to face the hardships of a literary career. He would have to start from the very beginning, and his hopes of material rewards, and of recognition, were extremely minimized by his own inflexible standards.

Until then his name had appeared in print only twice: once immediately preceding his suicide attempt in May, 1845, when *L'Artiste* published his sonnet "A une dame créole," and once when his *Salon de 1845* came out in pamphlet form. When he resumed his activities at the end of that year, he was obviously working steadily: his essays and articles followed each other in rapid succession in various newspapers and reviews. They appeared mainly in *L'Artiste* and in the *Corsaire-Satan.* In the offices of *L'Artiste,* which had been taken over by Arsène Houssaye in 1844, he rejoined his earlier literary acquaintances: Théophile Gautier, Gérard de Nerval, Banville and Esquiros. There he also met a beginner, a young man of his own age by the name of Champfleury. Champfleury's artistic principles were opposed to those of Banville and Gautier, and he felt more at home in the offices of the *Corsaire-Satan,* to which he was a regular contributor, than he did at *L'Artiste.*

Ever since the days of the Bailly Student Home, Baudelaire had occasionally dropped an article into the box belonging to the former *Corsaire.* The latter, which had been amalgamated with Pétrus Borel's *Satan,* was now—under its new title—pursuing the career which Champfleury later depicted in *Les Aventures de Mademoiselle Mariette* (The Adventures of Mademoiselle Mariette). Its contributors were for the most part young men of no means who led difficult lives in the sordid side streets of the Latin Quarter. Through Champfleury and Murger, who was also associated with the *Corsaire-Satan,* Baudelaire met a gifted story-teller, Barbara, the songwriter Pierre Dupont, the painters Bonvin and Courbet, as well as the entire fanciful and half-starved crew described by Murger in his *Scènes de la vie de bohême* (Scenes from Bohemian Life).

The undistinguished sentimentality and haphazard manners which marked the group could not meet with the approval of the refined dandy, whose fastidious nature had not been shaken by the severest trials and who had a constant hatred of laxity, be it of dress, feelings, or thought. But these novel surroundings served to enrich his experiences and thoughts. He saw, undoubtedly for the first time, privation, want, and suffering. His finances were so badly managed that, despite the fact that he did have a small income, he sometimes had to go without eating for two days at a time, or he would sometimes have to remain in bed, due to a lack of clothes or of firewood. The resources of his associates were even more uncertain. Their art itself was influenced by their living conditions. They were not interested in purely formal experiments and even less interested in the neo-hellenism or neo-paganism of men like Banville, or Louis Ménard. They preferred to cling to immediate realities, even when they were hideous, and they attempted to portray the circumstances of their lives as faithfully as possible. This was the "slice of life" theory of aesthetics and almost the formula itself, since in *Les Aventures de Mademoiselle Mariette,* the author said about Murger: "From time to time he cut an incident from his life as he would a slice of pâté and carried the same to Monsieur de Saint-Charmay, who happily accepted these biographies of poets and shop girls."

This group was later to formulate the doctrine of Realism, championed mainly by Champfleury in the novel, and Courbet in painting. Baudelaire's spirituality made him unable to adopt their methods. However, their aversion to all false idealizations satisfied an innate need of his, and it is likely that his association with them hastened his break with the School of Art for Art's Sake which had previously attracted him. He never ceased to admire the best practitioners of that school. He remained in agreement with them that form demands careful and painstaking attention, and deplored the slackness of a Champfleury and the commonplace subjects of Bonvin's, and even Courbet's, canvasses. But his respect for truth saved him from hyberbolic and exaggerated poetry: the pagan materialism which it expressed offended his mysticism. Neither of these opposing schools totally satisfied him. He borrowed from each elements which were apparently contradictory, but which complemented each other within his own aesthetic framework. The attacks which he launched against the *École païenne* in 1851 and 1852, and against Realism in 1855, were not recantations, or even signs of wavering, but were instead clarifications or corrections intended to eliminate such ambiguities as had been brought about by personal sympathy and a few common ideas.

The term "Realism" was itself no more than a label of convenience. Champfleury himself used it only with this understanding, and did not refrain, along with Courbet, from denouncing its conventionality. The word only vaguely characterizes the works of its self-styled partisans, whose imaginations smacked of Hoffmann, that least realistic of story-tellers. Baudelaire himself saw in Hoffmann much more than a fanciful lover of eccentricities: he admired him as a poet endowed with a sense of universal unity and harmony: a sense of Correspondences. If Baudelaire cultivated an interest in the fantastic, he did so for the light which he felt that it cast upon the invisible world, by dispelling the mist which hides that world from us. Baudelaire's first acquaintance with Hoffmann, who had become quite fashionable after 1830, was made without the aid of Champfleury and his friends. But his contact with this group served to rekindle his interest. Through them, he was able to gain a surer and more precise knowledge of Hoffmann. Champfleury had dipped into his sources, and was to publish some years later a whole series of studies on Hoffmann as an introduction to his *Contes posthumes* (Posthumous Tales).

One reason why both Champfleury and Barbara were drawn to Hoffmann was the role which music played in his life and works. Both were accomplished musicians. They initiated Baudelaire into this sphere, and music inspired a number of his most beautiful prose and verse pieces. This is a point of some interest, for the poetry written in France after 1830—especially that which evolved under Gautier's influence—remained aloof from musical influences, and sought plastic effects instead. Of course, this trend did not include everyone: Gérard de Nerval, for instance, went his own way. But Baudelaire's education and natural temperament predisposed him toward visual or plastic imagery, and it is an event of some significance that he was made aware at this time of the importance of music. There may be a predominance of visual rather than auditory imagery in his poetry, but, except for some early pieces, the effects which he actually sought were primarily musical ones.

Contact with Champfleury's group did not prove useless to him even in the realms of painting, sculpture, and engraving, where he needed neither encouragement nor initiation. It increased his opportunities for casually penetrating into the studios of the artists and closely observing their techniques and processes. Naturally he did not associate exclusively with his new acquaintances. No one could have been more faithful to his earlier friends; he was not a man who formed allegiances lightly. But in Champfleury, Barbara, Murger, and Pierre Dupont, he acquired true friends, who contributed a great deal to his development. His spiritual life seems to have been transformed as a result. Surrounded by these courageous and spirited youths, he experienced a new burst of confidence and enthusiasm. His productions of 1846 have a healthy, vigorous, and optimistic air. This group disdained artifice and exterior polish; they helped him to re-evaluate the role of craftsmanship in a work of art. "Celebrated poetic works are essentially stupid. That is what constitutes their power and glory," he stated in his criticism of *Prométhée délivré* (Prometheus Delivered) by Louis Ménard. His "Choix de maximes consolantes sur l'amour" (A Selection of Comforting Maxims about Love) states again: "Naïveté is what redeems, naïvete is what brings happiness. What matter if your mistress be as ugly as old Mab, the queen of horrors?"

In this work, he also warned against the usual clichés: "In matters of love, beware of the moon, the stars, beware of Venus de Milo, of lakes, guitars, of rope-ladders, and of fairy tales—though they be written by Apollo himself!" In his "Conseils aux jeunes littérateurs" (Advice to Young Men of Letters), he affirms the efficacy and excellence of will-power: "If you have a run of bad luck, it is because you yourself are deficient." He recommended persistence: "Debauchery is no longer a sister to inspiration." Inspiration was instead "a sister of daily work." He warned against an irregular private life: "Never resort to creditors; pretend, if it please you, to have them. That is all the advice I can offer." Finally he proclaimed an edifying—if somewhat naïve—confidence in the material rewards of poetry: "Poetry is one of the most lucrative of arts; but it is a type of investment which yields abundant interest only with time."

Baudelaire was evidently thinking of himself when he wrote these lines. Though he published only two poems in the whole course of this year (1846), we are informed by his close friends that he already had a good many others in his notebooks. In 1845 he announced the planned publication of *Les Lesbiennes, poésies* (The Lesbians, a book of verse). This was the title for a handful of Baudelaire's poems. It seems to have been chosen chiefly for its shock value, as was the title of Pétrus Borel's *Contes immoraux*. Baudelaire was still very sympathetic to the second generation of the Jeune-France movement. Indeed, he never did become completely disengaged from this group. *Les Lesbiennes* was the counterpart of Samuel Cramer's *Orfraies*

(Ospreys), that "collection of sonnets which we have all read or written when our hair was long and our common sense was short."

Samuel Cramer was the principal character of *La Fanfarlo*, a short story published in 1847. Baudelaire seems to have begun writing it in 1843. Since "Le Jeune Enchanteur" (The Young Magician), published during the preceding year, was a translation from English, *La Fanfarlo* represents his only completed work of fiction. This short story provides us with a portrait of the author, in the person of the hero. The picture is drawn with charm and humor: "Samuel had a pure and noble brow, eyes like translucent drops of coffee, a bantering and teasing nose, shameless and sensuous lips, jaws square and unyielding, and an exaggeratedly Raphaelesque hair style." This description helps us to arrive at an "assessment of Baudelaire," both literary and psychological, at a time when he was bidding goodbye to his youth. The evaluation was not sparing: "The sun of idleness which shone forth constantly within him evaporated and absorbed that portion of genius with which heaven had blessed him." Baudelaire wonderfully characterized "that sombre nature shot through with sudden flashes of light—lazy and ambitious at the same time—abounding in elaborate schemes and ludicrous failures." He grasped all of his own contradictions. His hero was "given to dramatization," but he was thoroughly honest in his feelings and his enthusiasm: "He fought a duel over an author or artist who had been dead for the past two centuries. Just as he had been furiously religious, he was now a confirmed atheist."

Samuel was a Romantic, "one of the last remaining Romantics in France." But his Romanticism was no longer the result of a spontaneous impulse. It was a reasoned Romanticism, wilfully arrived at, and not overdone. He is a Romantic who derides "his own Romantic jargon." He condemns all idealizations and illusions. "What is most disheartening is that all love meets a bad end, and the more sublime and soaring it is at the start, the more disastrous will it be at the finish."

The plot of the story is sentimental, and it resolves into platitude. The fact that some of its features are derived from Balzac is not important: the theme is definitely not typical of him. It is of an entirely psychological nature, and concerned more with the aesthetic than the fictional. The real substance of the story is Samuel Cramer's literary development. He moves from the kind of Jeune-France Romanticism exemplified in the *Orfraies,* to an output governed by necessity, to which he cynically applies the motto: *Auri sacra fames.* We need not point out that this degradation did not occur in the case of Baudelaire, though at times he gave way to pressing material needs. This explains his collaboration in the *Mystères galans des Théatres de Paris* in 1844, and, with Banville and Vitu, in *Le Salon caricatural* (The Salon of Caricature), and in "Causeries" (Conversations), which appeared in *Le Tintamarre,* in 1846. These were unsigned texts which did not involve Baudelaire's artistic integrity. On the other hand, Samuel Cramer's development and spiritual disintegration through material success are open to complex interpretations: they represent a lucid examination of Baudelaire's own weaknesses, a warning intended for himself.

The most significant passages are undoubtedly those in which he elucidates the aesthetic principles of his hero—in other words, his own. Not only are his affinities clearly revealed, but also his basic quarrel with Gautier's plastic conception of poetry and with the doctrine of Art for Art's Sake. Samuel gives evidence of a pronounced aesthetic sensuality, which revels in the interplay of line and color. "In him, love manifested itself not so much in the senses as through the intellect. It was, above all, an appreciation of, and an appetite for, beauty." These lines could be equally true of the hero of *Mademoiselle de Maupin.* But there is a scene common to both works, in which the two aesthetic systems can be compared. In Gautier's novel, Albert's supreme moment occurs when Rosalinde unveils herself in his presence, revealing her dazzling statuesque beauty. At this moment he indulges in a prolonged moment of contemplation, as if before a work of art. La Fanfarlo also reveals herself to Samuel, "in the sacred radiance of her nudity." Baudelaire seems to have had *Mademoiselle de Maupin* in mind when he added, "Where is the man who would not give half of his life to behold his ideal, his supreme ideal, appear before him in the flesh, while the idolized phantom of his imagination loosens one by one the garments which were meant to conceal her from vulgar eyes? But behold Samuel, who, taken with a strange turn of mind, began to scream like a spoiled child: 'I want Columbine, give me back my Columbine; give her back to me as she was the night that she appeared and drove me mad with her wild attire and mountebank's shirt!' " In spite of his awareness of the visual, Baudelaire could not conceive of beauty devoid of emotion—without the human element. This is the way in which the final episode of the scene should be interpreted. The chambermaid is sent off to the theater at three o'clock in the morning to satisfy Samuel's whim, who, "taken with a new idea, began to pull the bell violently and shouted in a booming voice: 'Hey! Don't forget the make-up!' "

The author elaborated upon this "characteristic trait" of his hero: "He would gladly have repainted the trees and the sky, and if God had entrusted him with planning the universe, he would probably have marred that also." Here Baudelaire put into words for the first time his propensity for the artificial, which has since been interpreted in strange ways, and which certainly needs further elaboration. He already hints at the supremacy which he was to attach to the human element. We come across this propensity once more in a passage from the *Salon de 1846,* where Baudelaire declared that "the primary task of an artist is to place man above nature, and to denounce the latter." One must not be surprised, therefore, when in contradiction to his earlier sonnet to Beauty, Baudelaire stated that Samuel "loved the human body as if it were a harmonious physical ensemble, or a magnificent architectural achievement to which movement had been added." He goes on to point out that "This absolute materialism was not too far removed from the purest idealism." These words clarify his preceding statements: they demonstrate that "movement" does not indicate simply a notion of rhythm. It was not merely an additional quantitative element, but a new *quality,* which is related to the realm of spirituality. We are reminded here of the uncertain aesthetic we found in the letter to Sainte-Beuve:

> Every mystic abyss is just two steps from doubt . . .

But is this really uncertainty? Is it not rather the painfully sharp perception of a mysterious conjunction of matter and spirit?

This aesthetic system achieves complete originality when it surpasses itself to include ethics. The artist is thus compelled to become an explorer, and a connection is established between art and the human condition. When Samuel Cramer defended his poems against charges of eccentricity and monstrosity, he contrasted his destiny and that of his "brothers" to the destiny of other men: they, in his words, "live to live, and we, alas! we live to understand. The entire secret lies therein. . . . We have distorted nature's significance, we have exposed one by one the virginal secrets with which our inner gentility was laden. We have reasoned like madmen who increase their madness by striving to understand it." It is difficult not to see in the foregoing the seeds of the Voyant (Seer) Theory, later elaborated in Rimbaud's celebrated letters. And Madame de Cosmelly's reply took on strangely prophetic dimensions as Baudelaire's life and work progressed: "It is true that you suffer; but it just may be that suffering is what makes you great, and that it is as indispensable to you as happiness is to others."

5 · *A Fondness for Pictures*

La Fanfarlo did not contain the first exposition of Baudelaire's aesthetic views. He had found an opportunity to state them by writing on those "plastic representations" to which he had been attached "since childhood." We can hardly over-emphasize the importance of the plastic arts to Baudelaire. He visited museums and studios all his life. He formed some of his closest friendships with artists. Among these we might mention Émile Deroy—with whom he at one time became so close that people spoke of "Baudelaire and his painter"—and Félicien Rops. Of all his contemporaries, it was Eugène Delacroix who inspired Baudelaire with the greatest admiration.

Baudelaire's essays on painting occupy a larger place in the body of his work than does his literary criticism. His first published pieces were the *Salons* of 1845 and 1846, and, between them, in January, 1846, the article on "Le Musée classique du Bazar Bonne-Nouvelle" (The Classic Museum of the Bonne-Nouvelle Bazaar) in the *Corsaire-Satan.* As soon as the *Salon de 1845* was published, the author announced the forthcoming publication of the essays "De la peinture moderne" (About Modern Painting) and "De la caricature. David, Guérin et Girodet" (About Caricature: David, Guérin, and Girodet). One may even suppose that he had gotten the first of these planned essays underway, and that parts of it were used in the *Salon de 1846.*

These essays, produced by a twenty-four year old beginner, show a surprising mastery, soundness, and wealth of ideas. They prove that Baudelaire had pondered certain essential artistic principles, and that he had already formed judgments from which he hardly ever departed in the future.

There was at least one question, however, on which he held conflicting opinions: the question of social and political institutions. The "Quelques mots d'introduction" (A Few Words of Introduction) with which he opened his *Salon de 1845*, were followed by a eulogy of the bourgeois mind and a kind word for "the enlightened and liberally paternal attitude" of Louis-Philippe. In the *Salon de 1846* there again ensued a clamorous dedication "Aux Bourgeois": "You are the majority, multitude and intelligence; hence you constitute power—which is justice." This was followed by a lyrical passage in the seventeenth chapter which invited the "guardian of public slumber, whether constable or municipal officer, in reality the army," to "maltreat a Republican": "Strike, strike, a little harder, harder still, my dear constable." These words, from the pen of one who associated with Murger, Daumier, and Courbet, one who was later to become a combatant of 1848, were indeed disconcerting. One cannot help contrasting these brutal lines to the rebuke which came from the same pen in the *Salon de 1859*. Then, he flung the following lines at the "hateful spirit of the bourgeoisie": "*Caput mortuum*, be still! Uncouth Hyperborean of former days, eternally nearsighted or rather scaly-eyed Eskimo, the vision of Damascus, all the thunder and lightning in the world, could not bring you wisdom!"

Can we trace here a complete change of allegiance in Baudelaire's political thought? Was he using the "right to contradict himself" which he claimed more than once? Whether a real change of allegiance had been effected is uncertain. What had prompted him to this aggressive conformity was precisely his excessive nonconformity. He was disgusted by all watchwords, as Champfleury tells us, "be they created by the army, democracy or journalism." During this last decade of the July Monarchy, the generally accepted position was that of opposition to the regime, sarcasm toward the throne, and sympathy for the Republicans, even on the part of the Legitimists. Along with this attitude we find that disdain of the bourgeoisie which always constituted a natural component of the artistic or pseudo-artistic mentality. Baudelaire needed no more encouragement than this to flourish an opposing banner.

Such declarations of political opinion, flung in the face of his readers, were not as foreign to art criticism as one would believe. During the Romantic period, decorative and ideologial conformity had been fostered by the artists themselves. Baudelaire protested against this peril in his own way, by calling attention to the fact that true genius has nothing to do with such immaturity. He subsequently gave up singing the praises of the bourgeoisie, but he persisted in denying the artist his purple patches and picturesque manners. In 1857 he was still writing: "Haven't you noticed that there is no one more comparable to the bourgeois than a genial artist at work?" And upon the death of Delacroix in 1863, he gave homage to the austere simplicity of his studio: "No rusty suits of armor could be found there, no Malayan dirks, no ancient Gothic scrapheaps or jewelry, no second-hand furniture, and no odds and ends: nothing which could have accused the owner of a weakness for those inconsequential trifles and rhapsodic flights which are evidence of childish delusions."

By means of paradox, Baudelaire was aiming, first of all, at a purification of the concept of art. In his actual art criticism, the validity of his pronouncements fills us with awe. It is probably safe to say that no other critic of the time made as few errors of judgment about the work of his own period. In 1845, it was a spectacular achievement to pronounce Delacroix, Ingres, and Daumier the three outstanding artists of the day, to place Corot and Rousseau before all other landscape painters, and to have intimations of Chassériau's genius. In general, he formulated opinions of the painters of the period which have remained true to our own day. But it was mainly by his critical methods and aesthetic principles that Baudelaire dominated the entire field of art criticism in his day.

His knowledge of technique, his constant visits to painters' studios, did not confine him to mere technical standards of judgment. He was able to establish the proper focus from the start. He also stayed clear of the opposite danger: the danger of losing sight of the specific nature of the different artistic forms, and drifting into literary or philosophic digressions. Philosophy, however, could not be dispensed with completely, as it includes aesthetics.

Baudelaire described very well what he felt to be his obligations as a critic: "Stendhal once stated somewhere: 'Painting is merely fabricated morality!' Whether you give to the word 'morality' a more or less liberal connotation, the same statement can be made about all the arts. They always constitute beauty expressed through sentiments, passions, and individual fancy. They all point to the variety existing in unity: the multifaceted nature of the absolute. Criticism borders incessantly on metaphysics."

He also attempted to solve the problem of favoritism: "In order to justify his existence, in order to have a *raison d'être*, the critic must be biased, fervent, and ingenious: committed, in other words, to a specific point of view, but a point of view which scans the widest horizons." This last imperative is not easy to observe, but Baudelaire complied with it effortlessly, thanks to his unparalleled open-mindedness and his remarkable versatility. He was able to take an interest in the most diverse conceptions of art and ways of thinking.

Many of his ideas were rich and stimulating, but he surpassed them when he defined the "ideal critic" as one "who is both entertaining and poetic"; in preference to one who is "coldly geometric," and bent on analysis. "A beautiful painting is nature reflected through an artist." The ideal criticism is that which shows this painting "reflected through an intelligent and sensitive mind. Thus, the best description of a painting may well be a sonnet or an elegy."

Criticism understood in this way is as creative as the art it endeavors to evaluate. It involves the same operation. However, while acclaiming Baudelaire's originality as a critic, we must also keep in mind the fact that he was much indebted to his eighteenth century predecessors, the Reverend Du Bos, Caylus, Diderot, and Falconet among them. He was also well informed about the lengthy open debates over the theses of Winckelmann, Lessing, Schiller, and Quatremère de Quincy, and he had carefully perused the works of Stendhal.

There are indisputable resemblances between Baudelaire and Stendhal, even though Baudelaire can, in some ways, be considered a kind of anti-Stendhal. This influence on his artistic criticism has been pointed out long ago. Some critics have even speculated that Baudelaire had abandoned his *Salon de 1845*—he did not include it in his plans for the projected *Curiosités esthétiques* (Aesthetic Miscellany)—because he feared that in this work his debt to Stendhal would appear excessively obvious. This hypothesis is certainly questionable. It is true that Stendhal's "position" when confronted by a work of art is very much like the one taken by Baudelaire. The effects of this position, however, are widely different in the two cases. Stendhal's observations are not those of an art critic. They are valuable mainly because they shed light upon the author's personality. Stendhal's plastic sensibility was less trustworthy than he presumed. It ends in his immediate sensation of pleasure, indifference, or displeasure. On the other hand, Baudelaire's perceptions were more far-reaching and he also had at his command a coherent and comprehensive aesthetic code.

In his *Salons* he usually contented himself with his so-called "criticism in the genuine sense," that is, an appreciation that does not hazard explanations. But he often indulged in the poetic and creative criticism we have described above. These more fanciful critical works frequently took the form that he spoke of: they became poems which he later included in *Les Fleurs du Mal.* The posthumous work by Jean Prévost, *Baudelaire, essai sur l'inspiration et la création poétique* (Baudelaire, Essay on Poetic Inspiration and Creation), clearly demonstrated the importance of the plastic arts in *Les Fleurs du Mal.* Indeed, an exhaustive study of Baudelaire's art criticism should also include his poems. Criticism of this sort transcends the usual characteristics of the genre. It is certainly an authentic form of creation.

Nevertheless, it is not feasible for us to examine Baudelaire's art criticism in this light in a book of this scope. We must merely note in passing that Baudelaire's art criticism was not a secondary, adventitious undertaking: it was an integral part of his poetic activity. Except for a few trivial and generally anonymous articles, Baudelaire never strayed from the main path of his poetic development. We have seen that for him poetry did not merely signify poems. It was a way of life and a principle of thought.

Even if we limit ourselves strictly to his aesthetic principles, we can only cover the most striking features. In some cases it is more convenient to refer the reader directly to the original text. This is certainly true of the well-known pages on line and color, and the distinctions between sketches made by colorists and those made by draftsmen. This subject, which Baudelaire first broached in the *Salon de 1845* in reference to Eugène Delacroix, was more extensively developed in the third chapter of the *Salon de 1846*. "De la Couleur" (About Color) was written with undisguised preference for the colorists, whom he called "epic poets." On the other hand, the "pure and simple draftsmen are philosophers and alchemists"—when they are not simply "colorists who do not make the grade." These insights are definitive contributions to the touchy and oft-debated question of the rapport between color and design, and they are formulated with the unequalled ease which Baudelaire brought to his critical essays.

Another distinction which Baudelaire made, and which was also remarkable for that period, had to do with the "two modes of understanding a portrait: through history and through fiction." Here we must avoid a possible misunderstanding: the approach which Baudelaire called "historic" must not be confused with photographic reproduction. Its necessary concern was that of obtaining a resemblance, but this did not exclude idealization. It is essential "to know how to give to each detail a reasonable emphasis, to put into relief all that naturally calls for attention, stress, and importance, while glossing over, and blending into the background, all that is insignificant." Here, indeed, we find concern for a systematic stylization, but one which exists for the purpose of arriving at a truth which is "historic." That Baudelaire never rejected this concept of a portrait is proven by the fact that he singled out, as the foremost representatives of this "school," David and Ingres, whom he appreciated, as his "Le Musée classique du Bazar Bonne-Nouvelle" amply shows.

On the other hand, he did not hide his preference for

the second mode of portraiture, "which is typical of the colorists." The concern of this method was that of "elevating the portrait to a painting, to a poem endowed with accidentals, uncluttered, and overflowing with imagination." In this mode, the painter no longer seeks verisimilitude, "and yet, as it often happens that fiction is truer than reality, so it can also happen that a subject is more clearly conveyed by the fertile and flowing brush of a colorist than by the draftsman's pencil." It seems likely that Baudelaire fancied a kind of synthesis of the two modes, for, in reverting to the question in the seventh chapter of the *Salon de 1859*, he declared: "An excellent portrait always strikes me as if it were a dramatized biography, or rather, as if it embodied the drama which is performed in the soul of every man."

In a period when painting was struggling against the inroads made by the newly discovered art of photography, Baudelaire assigned the superior role to the painter. The latter was the interpreter of truth, rather than of reality. This conception of truth, for which he used the term "the ideal," he opposed to the "fashionable" and the "trite," that is to say, to conventional tradition. "The ideal, that is to say, the individual rectified by the individual, reconstructed and restored through the medium of the brush or the chisel to the cogent verity of its inherent harmonious structure." This definition is certainly reminiscent of the "*Beau idéal*" to which Stendhal refers, and which he borrowed from Quatremère de Quincy. Baudelaire anticipated the pre-Raphaelites and the return to the primitive sources of art when he wrote that "art is turning back to its childhood to regain perfection."

The role Baudelaire attributed to "craftsmanship" was not a predominant one. When he contrasted Delacroix and Victor Hugo, Baudelaire called our attention to the fact that his observations were not applicable merely to the plastic arts. His discretion and modesty prevented his making any comments or explanations about his own work. He rarely referred to it, and, when he did, he employed such ambiguous and ironic language that all interpretations become risky. But when he spoke of others, and especially when he elucidated a discipline other than his own, he revealed his Poetics. It then becomes evident what a minimal sway the doctrine of Art for Art's Sake had exercised over him, and how swiftly he overcame it, expounding, instead, with perfect lucidity, his belief in "naïveté," the artist's supreme virtue. "The naïveté of a genius must be understood to comprise a thorough knowledge of his craft, plus the *gnôti séauton.* And his unassuming knowledge must take a secondary role, and leave the lion's share to temperament." *(Salon de 1846)*

Diderot was one of the first to proclaim naïveté an indispensable component of genuine beauty. Schiller proclaimed its value in poetry, and though Stendhal did not often use the term, it was the quality which moved him more often than any other. Baudelaire's insistence upon this quality was significant. He did not treat it lightly, but came back to it over and over again, always affirming the inferiority of craftsmanship to what he called temperament, and sometimes soul.

Here again, he associated himself with an idealistic philosophy of aesthetics, in contrast to the sensuality fostered by Locke and his disciples. This was a definitive stand, and one we should not lose sight of, if we are to comprehend *Les Fleurs du Mal.* The true creator must be able to maintain the proper proportion between craft and naïveté. In stressing this point, Baudelaire exposed one of Victor Hugo's shortcomings: "Monsieur Victor Hugo, whose grandeur I would not want to underestimate, is a more skillful craftsman than he is an inventive one. He is a more accurate laborer than he is a creative one. Delacroix is essentially creative, though at times he is clumsy." To Baudelaire, Victor Hugo seemed an impeccable craftsman, but he left nothing to the imagination. "He took such a pleasure in displaying his dexterity, that he did not omit one blade of grass, or the glimmer of one streetlamp." Delacroix, on the other hand, opened "profund avenues to the most restless imagination." (*Salon de 1846*)

It was also in reference to the plastic arts, in his *Salon de 1846*, that Baudelaire expounded his Theory of Correspondences for the first time. He quoted a passage from Hoffmann (the recognized source of the famous sonnet, "Correspondances," published in 1857, since it contains the evocation of the "profound and somber strains of the oboe," suggested by a flower scent). But the idea of Correspondences did not originate in

Hoffmann either: its beginnings and practice date back to Antiquity. Baudelaire's sonnet retains its beauty as well as its importance; however, its importance is not that of a discovery.

The reader has no doubt noticed that we have not followed chronological order in our study of the *Salons*. Our purpose has not been to analyse these works in their entirety, but to highlight the components of the aesthetic code, which was already present, and which Baudelaire was later to develop. For this reason, we are only now considering the most important points, which Baudelaire treated at the beginning and end of the *Salon de 1846*. These are not preoccupations of a purely artistic nature, but genuine declarations of principle. However, we must interpret them with some consideration for Baudelaire's unconventional use of words.

This task becomes even more difficult when we have to define a term as ambiguous as Romanticism. Baudelaire himself faced this problem in the second chapter of the *Salon de 1846*. Since he declared that Romanticism was his literary faith, it is of major importance to us to know exactly what he meant by it. The problem is not a simple one, for as Baudelaire himself stated, "there is evidently a contradiction between the word and the work of its principal exponents." These we can surmise to have been Lamartine, Victor Hugo, and Musset, although Baudelaire does not mention them by name. Evidently, he attributed a meaning to the word "Romanticism" which is not to be found in textbooks. We can trace this meaning further if we notice his allusions in "Le Musée classique du Bazar Bonne-Nouvelle" to "the false school of Romanticism" on one hand, and to the "austere school of Romanticism, that expression of contemporary society," on the other. This is a distinction of central importance, for it leads us to infer that when Baudelaire appeared to condemn Romanticism he was referring to the "false school," claiming instead connection with its "austere school."

In the *Salon de 1846*, Baudelaire's point of departure from Stendhal's aesthetic was Stendhal's declaration, in his famous definition of "Racine and Shakespeare," that: "By Romanticism may be understood the art of presenting to the public literary works which, through the present evolution of their mores and standards, are likely to provide the maximum of pleasure." Baudelaire likewise rejected the traditional definition: "Romanticism is in no way determined by choice of subject matter, nor by an absolute conformity to truth, but by a manner of feeling." This "manner of feeling" must, above all else, be anchored in the times: "For me, Romanticism means the most current, the most pertinent, expression of the beautiful." While Stendhal was satisfied with his general proposition, which he made in a half-joking manner, Baudelaire proceeded to specific statements, which reveal the essential traits of his entire poetic production in a few words. "Romanticism is another way of referring to modern art. It indicates intimacy, spirituality, color, and an aspiration towards the infinite, communicated through all the means available to art." The one quality absent from this list was melancholy, another basic ingredient of modern art, since it is what made of Delacroix "the most authentic painter of the nineteenth century." Even before Baudelaire arrived at the term "modernity," he felt that the artist must express not only the sensibilities, but also the forms of beauty, typical of his time. He terminated his two *Salons* with the same plea, which he made even stronger the second time, that the artist be capable of conveying "the heroic quality of modern times."

He had been dreaming of a "painter of modern life" since 1845: that "genuine painter, capable of wringing epic forces from our present existence, of making us see and understand, through forms and colors, how noble and touching we are in our neckties and polished boots." Such a man materialized in Constantin Guys, to whom he consecrated his last major work of criticism, which appeared in 1863. In the realm of literature, he could already hail Balzac, for whom he expressed deep reverence. He never mentioned poetry, in spite of the fact that most of his poems had already been written. Ten more years of ripening were necessary before the confrontation between the suspicious and confused public and the genuine "poet of modern life."

6 · *Action and Dreams*

IT IS THE GENERAL CONSENSUS that Baudelaire's life was a network of incoherence and nonsense worthy of *Scènes de la vie de bohème.* When his biographers come to the Revolution of 1848, they usually describe a boasting and gesticulating Baudelaire, whose revolutionary activities were confined to shouting on the street corners: "Let's assassinate General Aupick!" This interpretation of the facts is based on testimony which is questionable on several grounds. Its source, Jules Buisson, often proved himself malevolent towards Baudelaire. Buisson admitted meeting Baudelaire "on the evening of February 24th," after the battle, and his version of the circumstances shows that he was not taken too seriously by Baudelaire.

Actually, the Revolution of 1848 marked a turning point in Baudelaire's life and thought. We must interpret the sneering remarks in the first two *Salons* with extreme caution, and must not mistake them for declarations of Baudelaire's political affiliations. When he commented on David's *Marat,* in his "Musée classique du Bazar Bonne-Nouvelle," he betrayed, in spite of himself, an apologetic but unmistakable sympathy for the Revolution. The confirmations of one or two of his contemporaries, and his avowed interest in Robespierre, remove any traces of doubt. We must also be careful, however, not to make the mistake of labelling him a partisan because of this attraction. He was not interested in political systems, but in Revolution. Asselineau remarked that "Baudelaire was fond of Revolutions," but added that he was not motivated by his "fervor as a citizen."

His revolutionary spirit was akin to that of Pétrus Borel and Théophile Dondey. It was a protest made against the existing order of things and the rejection

> Of a world in which action is not the sister of dreams.

His was a metaphysical, as well as a social, revolt. But it was social, because he was profoundly sympathetic to poverty and suffering. Marcel Proust did not err in observing that "this poet who seemed to be inhuman and to have awkward aristocratic pretensions, was in reality the most compassionate and tender-hearted, the most human, the most 'democratic' of poets." Baudelaire's contacts with Daumier, Courbet, Toubin, and Pierre Dupont had sharpened his awareness and sensitivity to social problems. His mind was made up, even before the upheavals.

The Revolution of 1848 was an outburst of spiritual enthusiasm on the part of the people. Its vague but heartfelt generosity found a strong response in Baudelaire's temperament. Perhaps he did not take part in the fighting from the very beginning, but on the evening of February 22nd, he saw a municipal officer sinking his bayonet into the chest of an unarmed revolutionary who was attempting to escape. "This deed of awful ferocity," related by Toubin, who also witnessed the scene, no doubt brought about the final shock. On February 24th, Baudelaire took his place at the barricades, gun in hand.

A few days later he became a member of the *Société Républicaine centrale*, frequented the clubs, and founded *Le Salut Public* with Champfleury and Toubin, selling the paper in the streets himself, dressed in a white frock. The fact that he brought some copies both to the Archbishopric and to Raspail is quite significant. This paper acclaimed Pius IX, exalted the religious sentiments of the revolutionaries, and made an appeal "Aux prêtres!" (To the Priests!): "Your master, Jesus Christ, is also our master; he was with us at the barricades, and it is through him, and only through him, that we have triumphed."

The spirituality which prompted his actions did not cut him off from reality. He was better acquainted with the social and economic problems of the time than the babbling popular leaders. His precise and pertinent queries often placed other speakers in difficult positions. Considerably deceived by these experiences, he quickly lost the few illusions he had maintained concerning popular leaders. Though Baudelaire may have been a revolutionary on impulse, he abhorred disorder—most of all in himself. In April he was on the editorial staff of *La Tribune Nationale*, a Republican newspaper with conservative leanings. This does not imply a contradiction. His conservatism did not prevent him from favoring the June uprisings which decided the outcome of the popular Revolution. "I have never seen Baudelaire in such a state," declared Le Vavasseur, who was not one of the insurgents, but who paid homage to his friend's courage and his disposition to "risk martyrdom."

Baudelaire's disillusion became solidified with time. He objectively analyzed the feelings which had animated him that February: "My frenzy of 1848. What was its nature? Desire for vengeance. *Natural* bent for destruction. Literary fanaticism; recollections of things read. . . . The horrors of the month of June. The madness of the populace and the madness of the bourgeoisie. Innate love of crime."

One should never acknowledge unchallenged his self-condemnation nor ignore the ancient Jansenism which had nourished his moral and religious conscience. His kind of Jansenism was far from being doctrinal. It manifested itself especially through constant feelings of guilt, which led him to search his mind for suspicious motives at the bottom of his most generous and innocent deeds. When his mother's unwarranted accusation forced him to affirm that he had always treated Jeanne Duval with forbearance, he modified this affirmation: "Since the woman was beautiful, one can suspect that my forbearance had selfish motives."

He proclaimed his faults toward others and toward himself on all occasions. We must keep this in mind when we examine the judgment he later passed on his behavior. "Natural bent for crime," "innate love of crime," do not constitute individual characteristics. It was human nature itself that Baudelaire attacked here. He certainly never pretended that he himself had escaped this congenital malediction. The conditions of war and revolution undeniably further violent and destructive impulses. That his reading should have nourished his taste for revolution was also inevitable. His "desire for vengeance" can easily be explained: not in his relationship to General Aupick, but in his relation to the established order of things, an order into which he could not fit, and where injustice reigned. A soul such as his always has a reason for vengeance. Later, he was able to judge from a distance all the errors and extravagances committed during the struggle. However, it would be wrong to interpret his participation as an irrational outburst, or as a purely personal action lacking ideological foundations. His adherence to the Revolution during the entire year of 1848, his journalistic activities, his excitement over the events of June, all went to prove that he was ready to die for the revolutionary cause, as Le Vavasseur saw so clearly.

After the deeds were over, the repression which followed proved a bitter lesson for him as well as for others. He did not immediately give up his participation in politics through journalism. Indeed, it is almost certain that he left for Châteauroux in September, in order to become chief editor of the *Représentant de l'Indre.* This newspaper had been founded "in defense of conservative interests." But Baudelaire, to whom the position was offered by his literary connections, was probably not informed of this. Another possibility is that both as a revolutionary and an admirer of Joseph de Maistre, the word "conservatism" did not hold the same meaning for him that it did for the directors of the newspaper. Whatever may be the facts of the case, his downfall as chief editor was said to have been occasioned by his adherence to revolutionary causes, and to his bizarre mannerisms, which were monstrous and criminal eccentricities in the eyes of the Châteauroux officials.

Information about Baudelaire's activities during 1849 and 1850 is extremely scarce. It is one of the most obscure periods of his life. He left for Dijon in December, 1849, for a stay of two or three months, either for the purpose of working in seclusion far from his creditors and the confusion of the capital, or for other reasons unknown to us. In the few letters we have from this period, politics comes up only once, in a choleric reference to a young "democratic eagle," and to the socialism practiced by the peasants. All that can be deduced from this is that Baudelaire had not yet reached the stage of indifference. We have further proof of this, in his reaction to the events of the Second of December, which he later made known in *Mon Coeur mis à nu* (My Heart Laid Bare): "I was enraged over the coup d'État. How many bullets did come close to me! And then, another Bonaparte! What a shame!" This indicates renewed participation in the fight, carried out with equal fervor, or more precisely, with equal furor.

This was Baudelaire's final concession to action. It repelled him from then on. "You will not see me at the polls," he wrote to Ancelle in March, 1852, "I have made up my mind. The *Second of December* has physically divested me of political concerns." This withdrawal shows that his activity had been of a political, not anarchic or aesthetic nature. He did not succeed in disengaging himself completely. "I have tried to convince myself twenty times that I am no longer interested in politics," he stated in 1859, "but each new issue fills me with curiosity and burning interest." There still remained within him "a touch of his former revolutionary spirit," as he confessed in a letter to Sainte-Beuve in 1862. He possessed also a Christian awareness of Providence: in the same passage of *Mon Coeur mis à nu* as that in which he mentioned his "rage over the coup d'État," he comments on the Emperor's "providentiality."

Though Baudelaire took an active part in politics, the word itself does not fit in his case. Not only did he not belong to any one political party, and endorse one political platform, but his singular qualities prompted him to play the role of a conservative in the camp of the revolutionaries, and that of a revolutionary in the camp of the conservatives. He had sought agreement with his loftiest principles in the realm of political action, and he could not envisage politics in any other manner. Disillusion was inevitable for him, or rather, a certain feeling of deception and disgust even when the Revolution had conquered. He was carried along on purely idealistic flights and this idealism, in spite of his forceful personality, bore the imprint of the times. No one could have had a more individual and at the same time a more "imitative" disposition, as Baudelaire himself expressed it. Like Samuel Cramer, no one was readier to identify himself with, and enthusiastically follow, those whom he admired, but only in the direction that his convictions already led him.

The idealism, which permeated his writings in 1848 and subsequent years, partook of the rhetorical though sincere humanitarianism characteristic of the epoch, and of the more or less vague spiritualism which combined "religion and philosophy." He himself had done this on his article on the *École païenne*. His sympathies were attracted to those writers who represented these tendencies, to Pierre Dupont among others, for whom he wrote an important preface to the *Chants et Chansons* (Hymns and Songs) published in 1851. He also felt an affinity with the political poems of Auguste Barbier, with Brizeux, poet of the lower classes, and finally with George Sand herself, "a very great and justly famous author." With time he was to develop a violent contempt for her, first brought on by his bitterness over her failing to grant a promised favor in 1855. For George Sand idealism too frequently proved to be a way of fleeing the exterior and interior complexities of life by denying their existence. However, even if Baudelaire came to loath the ideas of George Sand, he never underestimated her talent as a writer.

Baudelaire had no illusions about Pierre Dupont, Barbier, and Brizeux. He was aware of their weakness as writers. But he found nothing to alter in his principle of 1846: "unassuming knowledge must leave the lion's share to temperament." By this time, his aesthetic system was taken over by a surge of spirituality. He openly proclaimed his break with the School of Art for Art's Sake and with the *École païenne*. To attribute this rupture to a supposed romantic rivalry with Banville—which seems to be disproved anyhow by Baudelaire's defense of Banville in a letter of March, 1853—would be to misinterpret the conclusions he had reached in the first *Salons* and in *La Fanfarlo*. These works leave us with a definite impression of his approach to the problem of form. When national considerations were at stake, a doctrine which isolated a writer from the times in which he lived and tied him to pure art, or to a study of dead civilizations, struck Baudelaire as intolerable: "The city is in confusion. The shops are closing. Women buy provisions hastily; the streets become empty, and all hearts are seized with the anguish of disaster. Blood will soon be flowing in the streets. You come upon an animal radiating bliss; he is carrying strange volumes of hieroglyphics. 'And which side are you on?' you ask him. 'My dear sir,' replies he in a gentle voice, 'I have just uncovered some extremely unusual facts about the marriage of Isis and Osiris.' 'The devil take you! May Isis and Osiris be blessed with many brats, but get the hell out of our lives!' "

Contrary to the opinion of many biographers, these lines were not aimed at Louis Ménard, who had not as yet proclaimed himself a "mystic pagan." In 1852, Ménard had just returned from the exile earned for him by his *Prologue d'une révolution* (Prologue to a Revolution), in which he enumerated the results of 1848. Though he was not in the direct line of Baudelaire's attack he was injured, or at least slightly grazed, along with his friend, Leconte de Lisle, his close associate at the time. The two who received the most piercing arrows were Banville and Gautier. This can be shown in Baudelaire's mention of the "childish dreamworld of the School of Art for Art's Sake," which, "by doing away with ethics, and sometimes even emotions, necessarily became sterile. It placed itself in violent opposition to man's genius." In his 1852 article on "Edgar Poe, sa vie et ses ouvrages" (Edgar Poe, His Life and Works), which was the first version of the "Preface" to *Histoires extraordinaires* (Tales of the Grotesque), he indicated Gautier almost by name, when he complimented Edgar Allan Poe for not having maintained, "as do certain partisans of Goethe and other cold marmorean poets, that all beautiful things are essentially useless." We recognize in the above words of Gautier's preface of 1832: "When a thing becomes useful it ceases to be beautiful," and again, three years later, in the preface to *Mademoiselle de Maupin:* "The only true beauty is that which serves no useful purpose." The reference to Goethe was perhaps directed at the preface of *Émaux et Camées,* with which Baudelaire must have been acquainted, though the book may not have been on sale yet:

> As Goethe, on his divan,
> Cut himself off from the world at Weimar
> And collected the roses strewn by Hafiz

So I paid no heed to the tempest
Which rattled my closed window panes
And, for my part, I composed *Émaux et Camées.*

This was only a few years before the dedication of *Les Fleurs du Mal.* But we can come to a better understanding of the scope of this dedication, if we acquire a more exact notion of Baudelaire's literary and personal relations with Gautier. Baudelaire had spoken of Gautier in barely favorable tones for some time. In the first two *Salons,* his manner was either condescending or frankly sarcastic, while in his article of 1846, criticizing Balzac, he was even more severe towards Gautier, whom he did not mention by name but designated as: ". . . heavy, lazy, and sluggish, devoid of inspiration, and capable only of stringing and arranging literary pearls which result in outlandish necklaces." Even at the peak of their relationship Baudelaire had serious reservations about "the gaps in Gautier's amazing intellect." Baudelaire admired him as a formidable technician, and as the author of brilliant romantic productions wherein he discussed the basic problems of human destiny. But, as early as 1846, when he wrote his *Conseils aux jeunes littérateurs,* he differentiated between Gautier's "often unimpressive serials" and the *Comédie de la Mort,* which he applauded for "its many charms." He looked upon Gautier's ideas with contempt, not manifesting the least sympathy for his aesthetic principles.

This period culminated in Baudelaire's total estrangement from the doctrine of formal art. He reached the point of extolling the doctrine of commitment, in the contemporary sense of the word, and of making it the primary requirement of art. He preferred the poet who "put himself in permanent contact with the people of his time, exchanging thoughts and feelings with them, which he rendered in noble and appropriate speech." He never deviated from this statement, from the time of the *Salon de 1845.* His response to those who accused Corot of not being able to paint was: "Those simpletons! Not taking into account first of all that a work of genius, or, if you will, a work of feeling, in which all is rightly grasped, rightly observed, rightly understood, and rightly conceived, is always rightly rendered when it is adequate." When we understand that Baudelaire already equated a work of genius with a work of feeling, we find no contradiction between the Baudelaire of 1845 and the Baudelaire of 1851, who said that Pierre Dupont's great secret lay "not in his technique, his ingenuity, or in his capacity of execution: it lay instead in his devotion to virtue and to mankind, and in that indefinable quality emanating from his poetry, which I would attribute to his boundless attachment to the Republic."

In this period, which we may describe as one of humanitarian exaltation and aesthetic optimism, Baudelaire committed himself to a degree he never had in the past. He proclaimed the usefulness, and even the spiritual utility, of art, justifying by this premise the most ordinary productions of Barbier: when the latter "set himself to promulgating the sanctity of the insurrection of 1830 in blazing tones, and of advertising the abject conditions existing in England and Ireland, in spite of his improper rhymes and his pleonasms, the question was settled, and art was henceforth inseparable from utility and spirituality." One of the merits he ascribed to Edgar Allan Poe (and this is hardly credible), in his unsigned "Introduction" to "Bérénice," was "the persistent notion of utility, or rather, a rabid inquisitiveness, which sets Mr. Poe apart from all the Romantics of the continent, and from all other partisans of the so-called Romantic School."

However, the involvement which Baudelaire required of the artist was not simply a political or social one: it was human in the widest sense of the word. In this same "Introduction" to "Bérénice" he places "probabilities, mental disorders, speculative sciences, and prospects for, or theories about, the afterlife" at the top of the list of "truly important objects of study, the only ones worthy of exploration by a man oriented towards the spiritual." Edgar Allan Poe's similar preoccupations earned "eternal praise" for him in the eyes of Baudelaire. His religious feelings were less specifically Catholic than ever before. They attained their most liberal formation and expression at this time.

The most serious reproach which Baudelaire directed against the School of Art for Art's Sake and the *École païenne*—which were extremely similar though not identical—concerned the threat of materialism which he felt imposed upon the salvation of the soul. "To surround oneself exclusively with the temptations of an art which emphasizes the physical, amounts to leaving the door to perdition open." In his letter to Fernand Desnoyers, in 1855, he also condemned the excessive attention paid to nature, on account of its sacrilegious implications. "You are well aware of the fact that I cannot go into ecstacies over a vegetable, and my spirit rebels against this singular and novel Religion, which will always possess shocking overtones for any man endowed with spirituality." Though his spiritualism remained somewhat vague, it preserved its Jansenist orientation: "I confess to all of Saint Augustine's remorseful reactions over undue enjoyment of visual beauty." On certain occasions he reached heights of religious eloquence, as in the first paragraph of his "Exposition universelle" (Universal Statement), which he wrote in 1855: "Although we find in nature plants which are less sacred than others, shapes endowed with less spirituality than others, some animals which have been more blessed than others, and however legitimate it may be to infer from the instigations of the vast universe of analogies that certain nations—being huge animals whose organisms have become adapted to their environment—were trained and destined by Providence for specific purposes of varying importance and elevation in the divine scheme, I nevertheless affirm their unvarying equality in the eyes of He Who is indefinable."

These considerations of Baudelaire's were closely related to those concerned with morals in the strict sense of the word. The initiate of the *École païenne* will be incited to "monstrous and unpredictable disorders." "He will have no perception of the useful, the true, the good, and the truly lovable." Identical reproaches were addressed to the School of Common Sense in his article of 1851, "Les drames et les romans honnêtes" (Genteel Plays and Dramas), where he attacked authors who had moral pretensions. He denounced, in the name of the same morality, the ambiguity of this falsely "virtuous" literature and of this art "fraught with dangers." "Such people as Berquin, Monsieur de Montyon, Monsieur Émile Augier, and others, are all alike. They destroy virtue." A notation of August 26, 1851 went so far as to establish a tie between morality and aesthetics, in more explicit terms than do those texts published during his lifetime: "Beauty will be that which guarantees the most goodness, adherence to the oath, loyalty in carrying out the contract, delicacy and understanding in interrelations. Ugliness will be equal to cruelty, avarice, stupidity, and dishonesty. . . . If the concept of Love and Virtue is not blended into our every pleasure, our every pleasure will bring with it torture and remorse."

We have now arrived at one of the landmarks of Baudelairean thought. On one occasion only, overcome by the burst of love and joy which Pierre Dupont infused into his hymns, did Baudelaire come to abjure, or at least alienate himself from, the great melancholy personalities of the first Romantic generation under whose spell his sensitivities had been aroused and inspired: "Recede henceforth, deceptive shades of René, Obermann, and Werther; flee into the mists of nothingness, monstrous creations of sloth and solitude, like the swine of Lake Génézareth go, and descend once more into the enchanted forests whence the wicked fairies have fetched you, sheep inflicted with Romantic vertigo. The genii of action leave no room for you in our midst."

This is the single and short-lived instance of such a recantation. His admiration for Chateaubriand, and for René in particular, underwent this one eclipse and remained intact thereafter. About other matters, the texts we have quoted could have been written at any moment of Baudelaire's life. He sometimes deemed it more useful to put additional weight on one of two aspects of his thought, and sometimes on the other but they were complementary, not contrary. The bungling inadequacies of Dupont and Barbier were to necessitate more serious reservations on his part in the future. On the other hand, he never lost sight of their spiritual qualities and temperament. His position on the delicate problem of utility and morality in art remained constant, in spite of appearances to the contrary. Believing in the effectiveness of the shock technique in the domain of literature and art, he almost never displayed his thought in an even light. He flooded with the strongest possible light a single idea at a time, leaving in temporary obscurity neighboring considerations.

This technique of concentration and surprise is quite effective. But it often misleads the reader who does not take the trouble to examine all the elements of the ensemble. This is why only a few writers have done work which can give rise to interpretations in total contradiction with each other, as Baudelaire did. During the same year, 1851, in which he produced the "Introduction" to Pierre Dupont's book, and the notation of August 26th quoted above, he also wrote the article entitled "Les drames et les romans honnêtes." In this article, he summarized the question in a few words, and clarified the underlying structure of his thinking. "Is art useful? Yes. Why? Because it is art. Is there an art which is dangerous? Yes. It is that art which upsets the conditions of life. . . . The first indispensable requirement for constructing a wholesome artistic system is belief in integral unity." The statement is complete. Art is useful in the measure that it integrates a particular conception of the universe. This stand is totally different from the doctrine of Art for Art's Sake, according to which Beauty contains its own morality and utility. Baudelaire differentiated between "wholesome" art and "pernicious" art. His compliment to Edgar Allan Poe for his "persistent notion of utility" is not surprising. He praises him, in "Edgar Poe, sa vie et ses ouvrages," for setting himself "the particular task of refuting what he wittily designated as *the great poetic heresy of modern times.* This heresy is that of proximate utility." The latter text appeared in March, 1852, and the former in April of the same year. The adjective "proximate" permits their reconciliation, especially in the light of the texts we have previously quoted.

Everyone was profoundly moved by the upheaval of 1848. It brought to the surface of Baudelaire's spirit some of its most lofty and idealistic elements, and strongly confirmed his identification with the social and spiritual distress of the human condition. All his writings were affected by it for several years. Later, he did not stress these points with as much urgency. The disappointments and grievances of his existence gave rise to more frequent tones of irony and sarcasm. But he was enriched by his experiences in the Revolution, and his human sensitivity survived intact, whatever screens he later employed to camouflage it. One could not find a more appropriate, a more beautiful and inclusive, summation of his poetic labors than that which he made in 1851: "Every true poet must be an incarnation."

7 · *An Adopted Brother*

THE YEAR 1848 was marked by Edgar Allan Poe's entrance into the life of Baudelaire. His translation of "Révélation magnétique" (Mesmeric Revelation) appeared in the July 15th edition of *La Liberté de penser*. This translation was published soon after his initial contact with the American writer, through other French translations which then began to be known. If we base our opinion on Baudelaire's "Introduction" to "Bérénice," it would seem that his first readings of Poe's work took place in 1847. In that "Introduction" he refers to the translations of Isabelle Meunier, which had appeared that year in *La Démocratie pacifique*. This date is also confirmed by a letter addressed to Eugène Pelletan, dated March 17, 1854, in which Baudelaire pointed out that he had been interested in Edgar Allan Poe "since 1847."

Many commentators have attributed considerable importance to the influence of Poe on Baudelaire's thought and work, basing their opinion on the poet's enthusiasm, and the tenacity with which he carried out the vast undertaking of translating Poe's works into French. However, we must interpret Baudelaire's infatuation with prudence. It is true that we can call upon many facts and documents concerning Poe. Five volumes of translations are in existence, representing fifteen years of more or less sustained effort in the course of Baudelaire's life. His admiration, formulated in no uncertain terms, was stated in the various commentaries which accompanied these translations, as well as in his correspondence. In the light of such evidence, some critics have posited a genuine infatuation on Baudelaire's part and have affirmed, as did Paul Valéry, that Poe's conception of aesthetics "was the principal factor influencing Baudelaire's art and ideas."

Such assertions call for a thorough examination of this question. The testimony which was most instrumental in promulgating this interpretation of the facts was that of Asselineau. He confirmed the thesis that the American author was made known to Baudelaire through the translations of Madame Meunier in 1847 and then went on: "Immediately after his discovery, he blazed with admiration for this genial mind, which shared so many similarities with his own. I have rarely seen a more complete, a more speedy and absolute, conquest."

Unfortunately the complete edition of the notes of Asselineau, which has recently been published, casts serious doubts upon the accuracy of his account. We find that actually Asselineau had seen Baudelaire "only on very rare occasions between 1846 and 1849." This second date is changed a few lines below to "I imagine 1850 (possibly '51)." Consequently, if Poe's conquest of Baudelaire was accomplished as swiftly as Asselineau claimed, he could hardly have been witness to it. Asselineau's honesty is unquestionable, and his attachment for Baudelaire continued even after the latter's death. But he only made notes at this time, and drew up a monograph dealing with these events twenty years later, and it is understandable that a certain amount of confusion should result.

The studies made by the American professor, W. T. Bandy, have now established the fact that, except for about a dozen tales, Baudelaire did not become acquainted with Poe's work until 1852. Before this date, he had not read either his poems or his theoretic treatises. He had become familiar with these works only that year, after the publication of his first important article, "Edgar Poe, sa vie et ses ouvrages." This article was, for the most part, simply a translation of two American articles. Baudelaire's aesthetic system was quite conclusively delineated by this time, as we have noted. It continued to evolve, of course, but further development occurred along lines already established.

As for Baudelaire's "confession," it falls far short of the scope attributed to it. The "unparalleled perturbation" which he mentions was not occasioned by a revelation, but by the discovery of a similarity between his work and Poe's. At one time, he even used this instance as an example of an encounter which could erroneously be interpreted as exerting an influence. No matter how striking a resemblance there may be, Baudelaire himself established its limits: "intimate resemblance, although not overly pronounced." And again, "I have devoted much time to Edgar Poe, because he resembles me a little." The publication of his first translations can certainly be taken as a sign of interest, but not necessarily of enthusiasm. The translation of "Le Jeune Enchanteur" shows that he had a liking for this kind of work and perhaps also that he considered this to be a relatively simple method of reaping a financial benefit from his talent. The admiration he expressed in his first introductions to "Révélation magnétique" and "Bérénice" was real, but not lacking in reservations. "The fragment by Edgar Poe presented here constitutes an argumentation, at times overly sustained, at other times obscure, and singularly audacious. . . ." "That he produced a few poor and hastily contrived pieces is not surprising, and can be explained by his deplorable existence." It is important to note that an interval of four years separated the two translations.

Without a doubt, Baudelaire's enthusiasm was increased when he discovered Poe's poetry and criticism. The work which seems to have held most interest, for those who have shared Baudelaire's admiration for Edgar Allan Poe, is the analysis of method and technique set forth in Poe's "The Poetic Principle" (Principe poétique in translation) and in "The Philosophy of Composition" (La Genèse d'un Poëme). The translation of the first of these essays was never published, although Baudelaire did draw upon it for personal use. In the second, we know that the author reduced the process of poetic creation to the exploration and systematic utilization of particular practices, without recourse to inspiration. The goal to keep in mind was not the subject of the poem but the desired effect, the subject itself having been determined by the means to be used. Valéry claimed to use an analogous method, especially in the "Cimetière marin" (Cemetery by the Sea).

It is not our task to examine the extent to which these techniques were actually put into practice by Valéry, or even by Edgar Allan Poe. But Poe's supposed influence on Baudelaire is based on these works, and it will be useful to find out what Baudelaire actually thought of them. In the course of his "Notes nouvelles sur Edgar Poe" (New Notes on Edgar Poe), when he commented on "The Philosophy of Composition," which had not as yet been published in translation, he made no secret of the fact that the article struck him as being "tainted by impertinence." But he gave us the key to the motive behind his gibes, when he added that such an article is beneficial "in spite of everything, for those in favor of inspiration foremost." As for himself, he was far from taking the essay literally, and deemed it as a calculated counterattack: "In the same measure that some authors feign abandon, aiming at a masterpiece with closed eyes, bursting with confidence amidst confusion, expecting the words strewn on the ceiling to fall and form a poem on the floor, so Edgar Poe—one of the most creative poets I know of—has injected artificiality in order to cloak his spontaneity, and to counterfeit self-control and deliberation." This interpretation is diametrically opposed to the one advanced by Valéry, who recognized in this "self control" and "deliberation" the source of Poe's originality.

Baudelaire saw in this essay nothing but an excusable and amusing hoax: "After all, a bit of charlatanism is always permissible, and not even unbecoming, to a genius." On other occasions, he called this the art of jugglery. "That aspect of the American genius which takes delight in a difficulty surmounted, in an enigma resolved, or a feat of strength executed with success—and which is compelled to frolic about with a childlike and quasi-perverse voluptuousness in a world of probabilities and conjectures, and to create *hoaxes* to which its subtle art lends the appearance of genuine truth." This art of the juggler is precisely what, in the eyes of Mallarmé and Valéry, lends interest to, and constitutes the superiority of, Edgar Allan Poe. They saw in this trickery a novel method, which supposedly animated the totality of Baudelaire's aesthetics. In reality, Baudelaire felt this to be the American author's weak point. Starting with his first introduction, that which accompanied the "Révélation magnétique," he singled out three traits which he felt typified the "unusual" novelists, placing Edgar Allan Poe in their midst: "1) an individualized technique; 2) an element of surprise; 3) a mania for philosophy." The first two were obviously related in his mind, for in order to explain the "element of surprise" he referred to "the preoccupation with the supernatural." He based "the mania for philosophy" on a perception of universal unity, citing the examples of *Séraphita* and *Louis Lambert*, and invoking Balzac's debt to Swedenborg, Mesmer, Marat, Goethe, and Geoffroy de Saint-Hilaire. His underlying ideas were disclosed in a letter to Sainte-Beuve, written in 1856. The letter listed for his correspondent the elements of a proposed article (which Sainte-Beuve never wrote). In it, he clearly demonstrated the true reason for his interest in Edgar Allan Poe. "The first volume," he stated, "was brought out in order to entice the public: tall tales, guesswork, hoaxes, and so forth." And he added a few lines below: "People will be inclined to consider Poe a mere *trickster*, but I will unremittingly emphasize the supernatural character of his poetry and tales. He was an American only insofar as he was a trickster. As for the rest, it discloses an anti-American frame of mind. He treated his compatriots with as much contempt as he could muster." If Baudelaire was lenient towards Poe's "hocus pocus," which represented hated "Americanism" to his mind, it was because he recognized in Poe the faithful echo of his own spiritual nature.

We have seen that his "Edgar Poe, sa vie et ses ouvrages," the first version of the "Preface" to *Histoires extraordinaires*, was based for the most part on indirect sources. Baudelaire's intuition steered him, with the minimum of error, to the root of what was to remain, for him, Edgar Allan Poe's dominant quality. He placed him among the mystics (a term which Baudelaire used in its widest sense), and proposed this moving inscription for his tomb: "You who have ardently sought to discover the governing principles of your being, who have aspired towards the infinite, and whose stifled emotions were forced to seek the dreadful deliverance offered by the wine of debauchery, pray for him. At this moment, his purified corporeal being is floating in the midst of the creatures whose existence he faintly glimpsed; pray for him who knows and sees; he will intercede for you." This is not a figure of speech, since ten years later, he reiterated in his *Journaux intimes* (Intimate Journals): "To say my prayers every morning to God, the source of all power and justice, to my father, to Mariette, and to Poe, as intercessors." He recognized that the genuine grandeur of Edgar Allan Poe emanated from the great spiritual heights which he reached, and from his "aspiration towards the infinite," which he posited as one of the chief characteristics of Romanticism from 1846 on. Valéry made no attempt to attribute Poe's influence on Baudelaire to this level of his thought, but related it instead to jugglery: the use of the clever devices, and the restraint, which he himself saw as appropriate to poetic creation.

Baudelaire himself felt this to be the lesser part of Poe's work. Nevertheless, he did not remain totally indifferent to it. He had written: "De Maistre and Edgar Poe have taught me to think." In his own fashion, he was extremely fond of restraint in art; he scoffed at carelessness, abandon, and imprecision. His perusal of the critical writings of Poe in 1852 helped him to define his own aesthetic principles. The violent reactions which had engulfed him during the events of 1848 had carried him far in the direction of "commitment." He had denied all importance to craftsmanship. He was at that time restraining a deep-seated inclination which had been in evidence since the days of the Norman School. The disillusionment he experienced after 1848 and the *coup d'état,* along with his decision to "alienate himself from all human controversies in the future" (as he wrote to Poulet-Malassis in 1852), reinstated in him a more balanced position with regard to the conditions of artistic production. He discovered the work of Edgar Allan Poe at this time, and it, too, encouraged a return to a new equilibrium, by providing him with the example of a delicate and scientific technique subordinated to spirituality. Poe even developed in Baudelaire a certain pretense to charlatanism. Such indications can be found in his projected prefaces, in which he prided himself on being able to teach in twenty lessons the art "of composing a tragedy which will not be hissed at more than another, or of writing a poem long enough to bore one as much as all the existing epic poems do."

His final observations were formulated after a total and

personal acquaintance with the writings of Poe. In "Notes nouvelles sur Edgar Poe," which he wrote in 1857—and developed almost to the same extent as the lengthy "Preface" to the *Histoires extraordinaires*—he summed up his thought on the subject. His attitude cannot be successfully defined from a few isolated sentences. Every statement should be judged in the light of its context. In his comments on Poe's "Poetic Principle," which he translated by paraphrasing it, Baudelaire once again condemned "the heresy of education," and proclaimed that "poetry . . . has only itself as an object." He specified immediately, however: "For the sake of not being misunderstood: this is not to say that poetry does not have an ennobling effect on morality, that its final results do not lie in the elevation of man to levels which transcend everyday concerns. The denial of this would be an obvious absurdity." Here, again, he condemned only the idea of *proximate* utility. He declared an unreserved admiration for the spiritualist: "From the bowels of a gluttonous world craving for material satisfactions, Poe took flight into the universe of dreams." And in re-working certain passages of "The Poetic Principle," wherein he included his own comments, he defined poetry as "the human yearning toward a superior beauty." The following paragraph, from Poe's *The Poetic Principle*, divulges the secret of Baudelaire's admiration for Poe, and, at the same time, it bequeaths to us Baudelaire's own definition of poetry, and of art in general:

> An immortal instinct, deep within the spirit of man, is thus, plainly, a sense of the Beautiful. This it is which administers to his delight in the manifold forms, and sounds, and odors, and sentiments amid which he exists. And just as the lily is repeated in the lake, or the eyes of Amaryllis in the mirror, so is the mere oral or written repetition of these forms, and sounds, and colors, and odors, and sentiments, a duplicate source of delight. But this mere repetition is not poetry. He who shall simply sing, with however glowing enthusiasm, or with however vivid a truth of description, of the sights, and sounds, and odors, and colors, and sentiments, which greet *him* in common with all mankind—he, I say, has yet failed to prove his divine title. There is still a something in the distance which he has been unable to attain. We have still a thirst unquenchable, to allay which he has not shown us the crystal springs. This thirst belongs to the immortality of Man. It is at

> once a consequence and an indication of his perennial existence. It is the desire of the moth for the star. It is no mere appreciation of the Beauty before us—but a wild effort to reach the Beauty above. Inspired by an ecstatic prescience of the glories beyond the grave, we struggle, by multiform combinations among the things and thoughts of Time, to attain a portion of that Loveliness whose very elements, perhaps, appertain to eternity alone. And thus when by Poetry—or when by Music, the most entrancing of the Poetic moods—we find ourselves melted into tears—we weep then—not as the Abbaté Gravina supposes—through excess of pleasure, but through a certain, petulant, impatient sorrow at our inability to grasp *now*, wholly, here on earth, at once and forever, those divine and rapturous joys, of which *through* the poem, or *through* the music, we attain to but brief and indeterminate glimpses.

Baudelaire paid only the slightest attention to the fantastic in Poe's work. He saw in it a phantasmagoria "akin to that of Hoffmann," and one which consequently did not contribute anything new.

There exists an ambiguity of emphasis regarding Edgar Allan Poe's merits, if we examine the attitude of Baudelaire and that of his successors. The latter were entranced by the aspects of Poe's work that Baudelaire himself wrote off as charlatanism. They said nothing of the spirituality which launched Baudelaire on flights of enthusiasm and brotherly devotion. This spirituality Baudelaire recognized as his own, not only in its positive form, as an aspiration towards the infinite, but also in its negative form, which was based on a sharp awareness of "the inherent baseness of man."

This is not the place for us to tackle another problem: that of the real importance of Edgar Allan Poe. We know that Poe is not overly appreciated in Anglo-Saxon countries. T. S. Eliot characterized him as a minor Romantic, somewhat behind the times, the American counterpart of Pétrus Borel. It seems to the present writer that most of Poe's tales, though expertly worked out, would not secure a prominent place for him in American literature. As for his poetry, it would be imprudent, if not impertinent, for foreigners to attempt to judge it more correctly than his own countrymen have done.

This question would be disquieting only if Poe had actually exercised on Baudelaire the cardinal influence which has been attributed to him by the critics. We have shown that this was not the case. However, Baudelaire was profoundly moved by this man, whose unfortunate fate struck him as resembling his own. He discovered in him certain ideas and conceptions of art which coincided with the essential points of his own aesthetic principles. He perceived a strangely fraternal spirit in the writings and facts at his disposal. Edgar Allan Poe's knowledge was beneficial to him because it confirmed him in the certainty of his genius, and the knowledge of his destiny.

8 · *From* Les Lesbiennes *to* Les Fleurs du Mal

BAUDELAIRE was hesitant to see his poems in print, and even more so to have them collected in book form. His enemies mocked him for having acquired the reputation of a great poet without having demonstrated his talent. In 1843, he withdrew his contributions from the collection of verse published by the Norman School. His apprehension over submitting to the public writings which stood a good chance of being neither understood nor appreciated, not only shows that he had a presentiment of the dangerous nature of his originality, but also gives proof of the typical doubting nature of the artist which had already come to the fore in *Idéolus*. From time to time his doubts led him to consider giving up poetry: "And if my book makes a big splash, what then? A play, a novel, even history, perhaps." It was in this vein that he wrote to his mother in 1851. On the eve of the first edition of *Les Fleurs du Mal,* he was still in the process of asking himself whether his poems would hold interest for anyone outside of a "tiny circle."

The lengthy delay in publishing this book (Baudelaire waited until the age of thirty-six) can be partly explained by other motives than his reticence. First of all, Baudelaire always had a "horror of pamphlets," as his letters to Poulet-Malassis in the beginning of 1857 asserted. But it was not only a question of the size of the volume or the number of poems. He wanted no part in a mere collection of unrelated poems, no matter how significant; this was probably one of the reasons for his final refusal to cooperate with his companions of the Norman School.

After the condemnation of *Les Fleurs du Mal,* he made a point of emphasizing that the book formed "a whole," and should be judged as a whole. He defined his thinking in even more precise terms when he sent the second edition to Vigny: "The only praise I hope for is that the book be acknowledged, not as a mere collection, but as having a beginning and an end."

To fulfill these requirements, a book must contain within itself an overall meaning, and be organized in keeping with a general theme. It appears that Baudelaire pondered the matter for a long time before coming to terms with himself and grasping the fundamental essence of his poetic universe. Signs of his hesitation can be perceived by observing the order of the poems within the various groupings as it changed between 1851 and 1861, as well as the variations which occurred in their titles. However, the interpretation of these titles is not easy. As Baudelaire wrote to Poulet-Malassis, he was "fond of mysterious and 'exploding' titles."

The original title affixed to his poems, namely *Les Lesbiennes,* belonged to the category of "exploding" or sensational titles. Though many of the poems dating from Baudelaire's adolescence are no longer extant, it is doubtful that they had any real connection with a title so obviously chosen for its aggressive character. The book was announced on three occasions, in 1845, 1846, and 1847. Baudelaire was then planning a collection of poems composed with the intention of shocking his readers as violently as possible. With the events of 1848, his frame of mind changed. He came to believe in the social and humanitarian mission of the poet. Jests and traps for the bourgeoisie concerned him no longer. Baudelaire switched from sensational titles to mysterious ones. In November of that year he announced the publication of *Les Limbes* (Limbo) and specified that "this book will appear in Paris and in Leipzig on the 24th of February, 1849." Although nothing came of his publication plans, Baudelaire stuck to this title for four years, and later planned the publication of this book for May, 1852 with the house of Michel Lévy, who had already been mentioned in the notice of 1848. We do not know whether he changed his plans because of a disagreement with his publisher, or because of the appearance that same month of a small book of poems bearing the same title and written by an obscure and provincial poet named Durand. Instead of speculating on this, let us acquaint ourselves with his purpose in choosing such a title.

A critic who was also a personal friend of Baudelaire predicted that *Les Limbes* would be a volume of "socialist verse." This interpretation is more likely than one would think, for the word "limbes" was a part of the Fourierist, or pseudo-Fourierist vocabulary, although its meaning was somewhat obscure. A preoccupation with socialism would not have been alien to Baudelaire's thinking at this time. "La Rançon" (The Ransom), which was included in a "batch" of poems intended for publication in the *Revue de Paris* in 1852, bore this comment, written by Baudelaire in the margin: "moderate socialism." This phrase referred mainly to the fifth stanza of the poem, which Baudelaire later eliminated. However, as the poems which were to have appeared in *Les Limbes* were, on the whole, the same ones which were finally included in *Les Fleurs du Mal*, it is unlikely that they ever had any political attributes. It would have been even more amazing had Baudelaire had socialist implications explicitly in mind. The term "moderate socialism" could not even have been applied to the note which accompanied the eleven poems published in *Le Messager de l'Assemblée* under the title of "Les Limbes" on April 9, 1851. The note described the forthcoming book as "a historical study of the spiritual perturbations suffered by contemporary youth." Such a "historical study" might certainly have proved instructive, but Baudelaire, of course, had simply used his own person as the source of his information. The meaning of the word "limbes" must be sought not in apocryphal theology, but in the contemporary texts in which it was used, for example, in the writings of Théophile Dondey, who defined it in the following terms:

> Neurosis, disease, hallucination,
> Whims caused by spleen and consumption . . .

We cannot evaluate Baudelaire's projected book on the basis of these eleven poems, but they do give us an approximate idea of what this collection of verse would have been like. The first few: "Pluviôse irrité . . ." (Angry Pluviôse . . .), "Le mauvais Moine" (The Wicked Monk), "L'Idéal" (The Ideal) and "Le Mort joyeux" (The Happy Dead Man), seem to be poems composed during his youth. Here, as in the productions of the Norman School, we find the themes of the Jeune-France, and those of poets from the epochs of Henry IV and Louix XIII, side by side with an acrid but scathing pessimism. If "Les Chats" (The Cats) seems far removed from those "spiritual perturbations" with which the poet promised to deal, "La Mort des artistes" (The Death of Artists) and "La Mort des amants" (The Death of Lovers) certainly express confidence in the attainment of man's loftiest hopes for an afterlife, and "Le Tonneau de la haine" (The Cask of Hate) also imparts a kind of moral instruction. "De profundis clamavi" (Out of the Depths) and "La Cloche fêlée" (The Cracked Bell) seem to relate to the depressions and misfortunes of life, while "Les Hiboux" (The Owls) terminates on a keynote of detachment which fairly well represents Baudelaire's spiritual condition after his political disillusionment.

The manuscript containing the twelve poems intended for publication in the *Revue de Paris* makes a more challenging study, as we do not know whether the existing order corresponds to the one in which Baudelaire intended them to appear. On the whole, they, too, were pervaded by an atmosphere of spirituality. But they also contained a cry of revolt—embodied in the "Reniement de saint Pierre" (The Denial of Saint Peter)—which will require further examination. This rebellion, too, was spiritual in its nature; it lodged a protest on behalf of dream, that is to say, in terms of the ideal.

We would like to possess an account of the "lengthy discussion" mentioned by Asselineau by which, on a particular evening at the Café Lambin, the title proposed by Hippolyte Babou, *Les Fleurs du Mal*, was finally adopted. The idea of "flowers" can unquestionably be attributed to Baudelaire. It had recurred in his writings from his earliest youth. The stroke of genius lay in combining it so successfully with "evil." The mere fact that this open debate occurred is indicative of the importance that Baudelaire attached to the choice of a title. "A great achievement! and God knows what a difficult one," Asselineau later reported. This title appeared for the first time under

Baudelaire's signature on April 7, 1855, in a letter addressed to the assistant editor of the *Revue des Deux Mondes* concerning eighteen poems planned for publication on June 1st. The adoption of the title necessarily implied a certain orientation in the character of the volume. But, sensational as the earlier titles and mysterious as the second one, it could be applied to different, and even contrasting, poems.

Baudelaire himself somewhat modified his intention with regard to this book between 1855 and 1861, though its basic concept remained the same. Henceforth its theme revolved around the problem of evil. The poems destined for the *Revue des Deux Mondes* seem to have been chosen for their forceful exposition of this problem. In the epigraph, which he took from the *Tragiques* of Agrippa d'Aubigne, and which was printed at the beginning of the first edition, Baudelaire anticipated the charges of immorality which were later to be levelled against him:

> They say that one must cast unspeakable things
> Into the pit of forgetfulness, into sealed tombs,
> That by the written word, evil, raised up again,
> Will infect the customs of later generations;
> But knowledge is not the mother of evil,
> And virtue is not the daughter of ignorance.

This defense is rather weak; in spite of its flawless logic, its applications are questionable. This is probably why Baudelaire abandoned the epigraph after 1857. The eighteen poems are themselves extremely pessimistic. After a series of sad or nostalgic lamentations, Baudelaire condemned love in a sequence of poems which closed with the sarcastic "L'Amour et le Crâne" (Love and the Skull). This poem was probably not meant as a conclusion. We have reason to believe that these eighteen poems were only the first part of a more extensive production, which was originally planned to appear in two parts, and which was to have included an epilogue. Baudelaire outlined this epilogue roughly as follows, in his letter of April 7, 1855: "Let me find my rest in love.—But no, Love will give me no rest.—Purity and goodness are revolting.—If you want to suit my fancy and rejuvenate my desires, be cruel, dishonest, dissolute, crapulous, and thievish—and if you do not want to be all that, I will kill you without passion. For I am the archetype of irony, and my sickness is incurable."

This epilogue was never written. Baudelaire expanded the second part into *L'Héautontimoroumênos*, an expression of his profoundly bitter attitude, but without the savageness of his original project. This outline displayed the most hideous defects of human nature with great cruelty. "A pretty collection of monstrosities," Baudelaire called it, "a *real Epilogue* worthy of the *prologue*. A genuine Conclusion." This is indeed the conclusion of a work dedicated to evil. The meaning of the entire book would have been too thoroughly concealed if the author had not also given us his prologue, "Au Lecteur" (To the Reader). The fundamental importance of this poem cannot be overestimated, for it alone endows the entire work with a spiritual and religious resonance. We do not regret that the epilogue as planned was never written. Its too brutal character would have only increased the misunderstanding to which Baudelaire is still exposed.

The public seal was put on this misunderstanding with the condemnation of the 1857 edition of *Les Fleurs du Mal*. As a result of this condemnation, a small fine was imposed on Baudelaire, and six poems were ordered removed from the work, because of their immorality. Baudelaire's intentions were not called to question, however, and homage was paid to his talent. In spite of the embarrassment of the judges, which is in evidence in the very wording of the verdict, three quarters of a century were to lapse before the indictment was revoked.

Baudelaire showed amazement as well as indignation at the condemnation. Though he had encouraged a certain kind of misunderstanding through his violent and ambiguous language, he had, on the other hand, clearly declared his motivations. He stated nothing but the truth when he emphasized that his book evinced "horror of evil," and that it "illustrates a dreadful morality." Notwithstanding the violent impact of some of the poems, the volume would not have misled anyone if it had been judged "in its entirety," as Baudelaire wished. The three concluding sonnets, collectively entitled "La Mort" (Death), contrasted with fervent faith the imperfections and miseries of this world with the rewards of eternal life. Finally, if, as Baudelaire himself stated, the book was "written with the intention of portraying the turmoil of the soul steeped in evil," the introductory piece, "Au Lecteur," clearly indicated the significance which he attached to the presence of Evil in the human heart.

However, both the phraseology and the arrangement of the poems were so full of ambiguities, that they could easily have misled the reader as to the earnestness of the author. One could have been thrown off balance even in the first part, "Spleen et Idéal" (Spleen and the Ideal), by the poems that concluded the section. The first three of these last six sonnets contained macabre and decidedly "frenzied" tendencies. "Le Revenant" (The Ghost), "Le Mort joyeux," and "Sépulture" (Burial) incorporated the most questionable extremes of the Jeune-France style of writing, and hence cast doubt upon the sincerity of the other "splenetic" pieces in the volume:

> And I shall give you, my dark one,
> Kisses cold as the moon,
> And the caress of a serpent
> Who crawls round an open grave.

The three sonnets which followed these, "Tristesses de la lune" (The Sorrows of the Moon), "La Musique" (Music), and "La Pipe" (The Pipe), offered such uncomplicated cures for the poet's suffering that all the preceding portrayals of distress could only be relegated to the category of fantastic and gratuitous imaginings.

Again, "Le Vin" (Wine), suggested as an effective means of escape following the formidable sequences of "Fleurs du Mal" and "Révolte" (Rebellion), considerably diminished their scope. To malevolent or unprepared minds, it vested the entire ensemble with a quality of pseudo-mystification. We may add that the observations that he made in connection with "Révolte," ambiguous and rather burlesque in style, were later decreed to be "detestable" by Baudelaire himself, and were not likely to help clear up the misunderstanding.

We must believe that Baudelaire had a certain awareness of these blunders, since he made fundamental changes in the arrangement of the poems in the second edition of *Les Fleurs du Mal,* and later declared the first edition to be "very inferior to the second." These changes did not occur to him immediately. His first inclination was to reprint the book in its original form, and simply to replace with others the poems which had been suppressed. This would have involved the publication of, as he termed it, a "second first edition." The notion of a total revision came to him only gradually.

If he adopted a more serious attitude toward his work and toward the public, and abandoned certain childish attitudes which he had inherited from the preceding generation, circumstances played some part in that change. When the new edition was just beginning to appear in the bookstores, Baudelaire was confronted with a new responsibility. General Aupick had died two months before. He faced the situation squarely: "This event was a solemn occasion for me, like a call to order." He considered himself henceforward the only person responsible for his mother's happiness, and he endeavored to surround her with affection and to avoid friction. The correspondence between Baudelaire and his mother was punctuated by "quarrels" and "violent reproaches" until the General's death. Only testimonies of affection are in evidence from then on; the sole complaints come from Baudelaire, who regrets that his mother does not comprehend the depth and sincerity of his affection.

This change in his circumstances filled him with a fervent desire to attain a more solid position by paying his debts and earning his living with regular work. He immediately made plans to join his mother at Honfleur, in the "toy house" that the General had bought and furnished to her taste two years before his death. Madame Aupick was to spend her last days there. At his mother's suggestion, they both decided to make it their permanent residence. Actually, however, Baudelaire was only able to spend a few months there, in 1859. The fact is that his circumstances were far from good, in spite of his good intentions. As his desire for order and peace of mind increased, he felt more and more disturbed by "the sickening and offensive contrast between [his] spiritual honor and [his] wretched and uncertain life."

We must understand this "spiritual honor" in the widest sense. It included mental activity as well as spirituality. However, the latter dominated his thinking more and more. It was evident in all his writings, and it came increasingly to resemble orthodox Catholicism. His theology had retained the Christian foundations of his earliest religious training: "Mystic tendencies beginning with my childhood. My conversations with God." When his childhood ended he seems to have preserved only a more or less empty framework of Christianity. In 1848 this early theology dissolved into the vague religious aspirations which were popular at the time. But Baudelaire's connection with Christianity was never broken, as his articles in the *Salut Public* attested. After 1855, the essay entitled "De l'Essence du Rire et généralement du Comique dans les Arts plastiques" (The Essence of Laughter and More Especially of the Comic in the Plastic Arts) indicates that he returned to the dogma.

Baudelaire did not commit himself personally: ". . . if one would want to adopt the orthodox point of view . . ." ". . . from the viewpoint of Christian philosophy . . ." Nevertheless, such caution cannot fool anyone. Not only did he cite the example of Christ: "To touch lightly upon the most sacred of remembrances, I will call to your attention . . . that the Sage of Sages, the incarnate Word, never laughed," but his statements borrowed the terms of theology spontaneously: "And notice that it is also with tears that man washes away the sufferings of man, and it is with his laughter that he pacifies and conquers his heart; for the consequences of his fall will become the means of his redemption."

The following year an important letter to Alphonse Toussenel concerning the Fourierist work, *Le Monde des Oiseaux* (The World of Birds), clearly marked his break with the "philosophies of 1848." The letter denounced "the great modern heresy, that of the substitution of the *artificial* doctrine for the natural one—by which I refer to the abolishment of the idea of *original sin*." It concluded with this meaningful statement: "All of Nature shared in original sin." This sentence throws light on the statement about Nature which he made in 1855 and from which we have previously quoted. All of Baudelaire's works testify to his awareness of Nature. His rejection of her was not akin to Vigny's. He rejected Nature not because of her indifference to man, but because she did not share in the struggle for salvation, although she had participated in original sin.

By 1857 we do not only find references to the dogmas of Christianity, but "to the Church, the divine Mother, who always stands ready: this Pharmacy where no one has the right to doze!" He said this in connection with *Madame Bovary!* Flaubert did not react to it then, but four years later, when he congratulated Baudelaire on his *Paradis artificiels* (Artificial Paradise), he could not refrain from raising an objection: "It seems to me that . . . you have placed too much emphasis on the Spirit of Evil. Here and there one gets whiffs of the leaven of Catholicism." His sense of smell did not mislead him, but Baudelaire was not the man to renounce his convictions: "I was struck with your observations, and having made very serious efforts to recall my meditations, I realize that I have always been obsessed by the impossibility of accounting for certain sudden human thoughts or actions without envisaging an intervening evil force, existing separate from man. This is quite a confession, but it will not bring color to my cheeks, in spite of all the assembled legions of the nineteenth century."

From 1861 on, he openly proclaimed himself a Catholic. He declared that *Les Fleurs du Mal* "was grounded in Catholic ideas," and wrote to Victor de Laprade that "he had always been a fervent Catholic." In 1862, in referring to *Les Misérables*, he directed the reader's attention to its "orthodox doctrine," "the true Catholic faith." In 1863, he wrote of Eugène Delacroix that "he returned to the fold of Catholicism through simple common sense." In 1864 he mentions his "manifest sympathy for the Jesuits," and in 1865 he made no secret of his faith and differentiated between *his* God and "the God of Messieurs Rogeard, Michelet, Benjamin Gastineau, Mario Proth, Garibaldi, and Father Chatel." On the eve of his illness in 1866, he wrote to Ancelle that his book on Belgium "is the mockery of all that people call *progress* and that I, myself, call the paganism of idiots."

These quotations help us to discard the tradition which holds that between 1860 and 1862 Baudelaire passed through a religious "crisis" which had no lasting effects. This tradition seemed confirmed when Jacques Crépet amalgamated with

Fusées (Fireworks) the eight concluding paragraphs of *Mon Coeur mis à nu*. There we find under the headings of "Hygiene-Conduct-Morals," some of the most fervent expressions of Baudelaire's religious faith. Until that time, it was supposed that these texts represented the final results of Baudelaire's religious thought. However, *Fusées* was finished in 1862. Biographers therefore concluded that contrary to previous opinions these paragraphs were an outgrowth of a fleeting emotional crisis. Some have even ascribed it to the debilitating influence of his illness. Upon close examination, we find that the amalgamation is valid for only two out of the eight paragraphs, and that of these the 1862 limit can be applied only to the first. The other corresponds to the wording of a letter dated 1865. Furthermore, there are many other paragraphs of *Mon Coeur mis à nu* which reveal similar attitudes, and the texts which we have quoted above prove that these attitudes persisted until the end of his life. We must add that the persistence of this faith was uneven, and Baudelaire experienced moments of doubt during this period of his life as in all others. But what concerns us is the feeling which permeated his work and determined his aesthetic principles. An analysis of his poetry would prove it enough, but its conclusions might be subject to debate, had the author himself not corroborated them elsewhere in such positive terms.

The dates we have established attain a certain significance from the fact that we are faced with three different editions of *Les Fleurs du Mal*. Besides those of 1857 and 1861, there was the posthumous edition of 1868 compiled by Banville and Asselineau, which contains a number of supplementary pieces. All these pieces had been published previously, except for the sonnet to Théodore de Banville. Jacques Crépet believed for a long time that this edition was based on a manuscript arranged by Baudelaire, and for this reason he followed this text in his first annotated edition of 1922. But subsequently he bowed before the objections which were advanced by other critics. Today it is an accepted fact that the edition of 1861 presents us with the arrangement finally established by Baudelaire.

A study of *Les Fleurs du Mal* would not be complete if we neglected the six banned poems which were eliminated against his will and the poems which he intended for a third edition.

Baudelaire never thought of composing a new collection of poems except for those included under the meaningful title of *Épaves* (Waifs), which contained his afterthoughts. These he did not even acknowledge; he wanted to create the impression that he had had no hand in their publication. He conceived of his poetic achievement as a coherent ensemble with a single title. Once this title was discovered he spoke no longer of poems, but only of "flowers," until his death. It is therefore essential to examine all of the poems finally destined for inclusion in the "unique framework" of the 1861 edition. That this edition is completely in accord with his wishes is demonstrated by a famous passage in his letter to Ancelle, dated February 18, 1866. "Must I explain to you, you who seem to have guessed no more than the others, that I have put my whole heart into that atrocious book, all my compassion, all my religion (travestied), all my hatred? It is true that I will write the contrary, that I will swear by all the gods that it is a work of pure art, mere monkey-play, a feat of acrobatics. And I will be lying through my teeth."

It is, therefore, the second edition which we will study, and which will unlock for us the hidden meaning and the fundamental aesthetic principles of *Les Fleurs du Mal*. But we can and must append all the other "flowers" which complete the collection of Baudelaire's poetry and fill out the repertory of his artistic resources.

9 · *Secret Architecture*

IN 1857 Baudelaire dedicated *Les Fleurs du Mal* to Théophile Gautier. In the dedication he expressed his reverence for the "Master and friend" with "a sense of the deepest humility." Five years after the appearance of *Émaux et Camées* and in the year in which Gautier published his reply "A Théodore de Banville" in *L'Artiste,* this dedication must have seemed a declaration of faith in the doctrine of Art for Art's Sake. In fact, the first draft of this dedication was rejected by Gautier because "a dedication should not be a declaration of faith." It is of interest to us to examine it now, precisely because it *was* a declaration of faith. In it, Baudelaire contrasted the aesthetics of *Les Fleurs du Mal* with the principles held by Gautier: "Though I call upon you to accept the role of godfather to *Les Fleurs du Mal,* do not suppose that I am so confused as to think that these stunted flowers are deserving of your noble patronage. I know that in the ethereal regions of true Poetry neither Evil nor Good exist, and that this paltry catalogue of melancholy and crime justifies the decrees of morality, just as the blasphemer confirms the existence of religion." Baudelaire then concluded by declaring himself "the most devoted, the most respectful, and the most envious of disciples," and pledged his faith many times over to his "godfather." That is, he recognized the moral significance of his own work, founded as it was on the distinction between Good and Evil, in contradistinction to Gautier's artistic principles, and he modestly refused to follow Gautier into what he calls "the ethereal regions of true Poetry." It is likely that here Baudelaire was making a concession to courtesy, or even flattery, and that he did not believe his book to have fallen short of "true Poetry" by abandoning those "ethereal regions." We might clarify the dedication further if we refer to the article of 1859, the subject of which was again Gautier. In it Baudelaire states that Gautier's muse "loved dreadful and forbidding landscapes or those that emit monotonous charm; the azure shores of Ionia or the dazzling sands of the desert." She "would run the risk of *not being visible and tangible enough* if she were not so supple and obedient, or if she were not the daughter of a master capable of endowing all that he contemplates with life."

Though his artistic position was clearly defined in this first draft of the dedication, his moral attitude was not elucidated. Baudelaire did not make it plain whether this "catalogue" was written for the purpose of glorifying or condemning Evil. However, the prologue, "Au Lecteur," dispelled all ambiguity. It made known not only his moral, but also his religious, attitude. In tones resembling those of the Fathers of the Church, and Saint Augustine in particular, Baudelaire affirmed man's persistence in sin, and expressly named the Devil as its cause. It would have been impossible to be clearer. His precision, his insistence, both exclude the possibility that we are dealing with merely poetic imagery or symbolism. This denunciation of evil is perfectly orthodox. Not satisfied with the use of the first person plural, Baudelaire insistently pronounces his own sentence, along with that of other men, in the last line:

—Hypocrite reader—my double—my brother!

This poem should have sufficed to eliminate all misunderstanding, even of a book that was exclusively dedicated to Evil. But this was not the case.

In the title of the first part, "Spleen et Idéal," Baudelaire placed, in opposition to "Spleen"—a word which corresponds to the "ennui" (boredom) which the prologue calls one of the most painful and cruel consequences of sin—the "Ideal": the "aspiration towards the infinite" which constitutes one of the essential traits of Romanticism. This was his way of designating the "two simultaneous aspirations, one towards God, the other towards Satan," which he found "in all men at all times." The title indicated that if the overall emphasis of the book was on the Satanic aspiration, the opposing tendency was not neglected.

The fact is that the first poems give off more light than darkness. "Bénédiction" (The Blessing) reworked and completely transformed a Romantic theme which was common to many poems produced after 1830. This theme, which can be found in the poems of Pétrus Borel, Félix Arvers, and Lefèvre-Deumier, is that of the poet's malediction: a malediction at the same time fertile, and therefore beneficial. Musset speaks of the artistic enrichment the poet acquires through suffering:

> Hymns of despair are the most beautiful hymns. . . .

and Vigny wrote, "The poet is accursed in life and blessed in name." This is not the place to question the sincerity of the above-mentioned poets. They broached the subject as men of letters and concerned themselves with the relationship of suffering to poetic creation.

Baudelaire's poem carries a different meaning. It is true that it, like the others, deals specifically with the poet. In fact, the 1857 edition of *Les Fleurs du Mal* is centered entirely upon the poet's destiny rather than upon common humanity. The closing sonnet of the volume was "La Mort des artistes." The book was transformed in 1861, not only by the addition of the thirty-five poems, but also because its new arrangement modified its emphasis and enlarged its scope. The poet necessarily remained its subject: *Les Fleurs du Mal* is for the most part the expression of an inner experience. But he became henceforward a witness to human life, and all readers, regardless of their *métier*, were affected.

The quality which arrests our attention in "Bénédiction" is its spiritual significance. It is not simply consolation or compensation which awaits the poet:

> In the blessed ranks of the holy Legions.

Heaven and earth are not two airtight compartments. The sufferings endured in this world will save him in the next; they are a mode of Redemption. This was not an innovation in the realm of ideas, but it certainly was in the world of poetry. Poetry thus came to be associated not only with suffering, but with the redemptive function of this suffering. In other words, poetry was a record of the spiritual struggles of man.

We can now examine *Les Fleurs du Mal* in the proper perspective. The next five poems deal, in diverse ways, with the same theme as "Bénédiction." They are concerned with the privileged character of the poet, which is related to his earthly malediction. The sonnet "Correspondances" is included here since it implies that the perception and utilization of Correspondences are privileges of the poet. But we must not ignore the primarily mystic significance of this poem. In it, the *synesthesia* or the Correspondence of sensations is attributed to the a priori existence of universal analogies.

The principle of universal analogies, originating in Plato, had already inspired countless religious and philosophic treatises. In the eighteenth century it became the object of a new surge of interest. The Swedish philosopher, Swedenborg, had attempted to erect in his works a rigorous and detailed system of Correspondences between the spiritual and the physical world. Martinès de Pasqually and Saint-Martin had further developed this point. Their disciples came from widely diversified strata of eighteenth century society, and later included such men as Joseph de Maistre and Balzac. Baudelaire also passed under the shadow of Swedenborg's influence, and remained faithful to his central idea of analogies, though he did not embrace the doctrine in all its ramifications.

The sonnet "Correspondances" is of central importance to us. It throws light on a fundamental concept in Baudelaire's poetry. But we must keep in mind that the source of its rich originality is its beauty of expression rather than its theme, which is not a new one. The mystical philosophy of universal analogies was centuries old, and its application to aesthetics had already been elaborated by Pierre Leroux in an article of the *Revue Encyclopédique* in 1831. Baudelaire himself had indicated the passage in Hoffmann which had inspired his sonnet. Though the sonnet expressed Baudelaire's conception of the universe, it did not deal with his conception of man, which is the true subject of his book.

"Les Phares" (Beacons) provides the best illustration of Baudelaire's concept of man. The eight magnificent "commemorative" stanzas of the beginning should not mislead us so that we neglect the last three, which give us the key to the entire poem. Baudelaire was concerned here with the role of the artist. Regardless of the form taken by each work of art,

> These curses, blasphemies, complaints,
> These ecstacies, these shouts, these tears,
> These cries of Te Deum . . .

it possesses the same universal bearing (echo) the same capacity for radiance and luminosity (cries, messages, beacons, calls), and serves as a proof of our dignity as men, or of our yearning for God.

The sequence of poems unfolds logically, according to a preordained plan. We can observe the emergence of this "secret architecture," which Barbey d'Aurevilly first pointed out in his article of 1857. We must study it further, if we are to understand Baudelaire's affirmation that this book "is not a mere collection; it has a beginning and an end." An overly detailed analysis is not possible here. At times the position of the poems is only approximately suitable, though the basic outline of the work never becomes blurred. After the series of six radiant poems which we have just mentioned, Baudelaire placed a gloomy sequence of poems filled with dejection, suffering, and failure. These are followed by "La Vie antérieure" and two other poems on the theme of escape. We can add that "Don Juan aux Enfers" (Don Juan in Hell) and "Châtiment de l'orgueil" (The Punishment of Pride) also represent an attempt to escape through pride; the second poem acts as a reply to the first. "La Beauté" then inaugurates a purely aesthetic cycle, terminated by "L'Hymne à la Beauté" (Hymn to Beauty). But we must not confuse poetry with aesthetic theory. Beauty can manifest itself in many different forms to the poet's vision. The validity of the celebrated sonnet:

> I am beautiful, O mortals, a dream in stone . . .

would be nullified by the total impact of *Les Fleurs du Mal,* if we try to see in it a declaration of principle. This "dream in stone" may have attracted Baudelaire at one time, but all indications prove that it did not captivate him permanently. "L'Idéal" and "La Géante" are also the poetic realizations of some of his aesthetic opinions, but it would be a mistake to ascribe a deep significance to them. "La Géante" in particular is nothing more than a symbolic reverie. "Le Masque" (The Mask) and "L'Hymne à la Beauté" furnish us with clearer clues to Baudelaire's thought. The former concentrates on the human aspect of art, which reveals suffering even when it attempts to hide it. "L'Hymne à la Beauté" relates art not to human ethics, but to the supernatural destiny of man. Beauty is a result not only of suffering, but of Evil, in the full sense of that word:

> You walk upon the dead, Beauty, and you mock them;
> Among your jewels Horror is not the least charming,
> And Murder, the most precious of your trinkets,
> Dances lasciviously on your proud breast.

The problem is a perplexing one: it is nothing less than whether Beauty has a divine or a Satanic origin. Baudelaire cannot conceive of an art devoid of "aspiration towards the infinite." "It is this magnificent, this enduring impulse towards beauty which prompts us to view the earth and all its phenomena as a glimpse or counterpart of Heaven." But as he sought "the definition of Beauty—of *his* conception of the Beautiful," he arrived at the conclusion "that melancholy is . . . her illustrious companion, so closely linked to her that I can scarcely conceive . . . of a type of Beauty which excludes Unhappiness." In his estimation it "would be difficult not to conclude that the perfect ideal of virile masculine Beauty is Satan, as Milton portrayed him."

It is evident, therefore, that he was not concerned with the ambivalence of Beauty merely as a poetic theme. Just as the human being aspires towards opposing goals, so art is inspired by Satan as well as by God. This is fundamentally a new aesthetic assertion. Until then the existing views of art could be reduced to one of two assumptions: art is either moral, or it is divorced from all moral considerations. Crébillon le Tragique is supposed to have said that since Heaven had been taken over by Corneille, and Earth by Racine, his only remaining choice was Hell.

Sainte-Beuve is known to have suggested a similar argument to Baudelaire during his trial. But this point of view, which is analogous to that of the painter in search of a "motif" who simply accepts the one he finds handiest, is too trivial to ascribe to Baudelaire. For him, the very nature of Beauty was at stake.

His theory can be more closely linked with that of the Marquis de Sade, who held that Evil is man's prime mover toward pleasure. The distance between pleasure and aesthetic excitement is not great, especially if one accepts Stendhal's statement that: "Beauty is but the promise of happiness." Baudelaire certainly did not intend to make the artist one of Satan's henchmen, or Beauty the exclusive product of Hell. But he was not content with illusions on this subject. Human nature being what it is, art, like any other activity of man, necessarily feeds on Evil just as much as on Good. Baudelaire did not answer his own query about the origin of Beauty, but the "no matter" attitude which emerges in the last two stanzas of "L'Hymne" does not point to indifference on the part of the author. As long as the power of Beauty is beneficial, and it opens the doors

> To an infinite that I love, and that I have never known . . .

it matters little whether Satan had a hand in it. This poem is important because it faces this question without hypocrisy and throws light on a subject too often abandoned to the shadows of ambiguity.

We must now embark upon the cycle of poems named after Jeanne Duval, which would be more appropriately entitled the "Cycle of Casual Love." In the first edition it begins with "Les Bijoux" (The Jewels), and in the second with "Parfum exotique." It has been proven beyond a doubt that not all the poems in this section were actually inspired by the mulatto woman. Some of them, of course, unquestionably refer to her. But we must put the question of identity aside, and study the ensemble as Baudelaire composed it. As in the previous poems, the Satanic element is often stressed—very much so in "Le Possédé" (The Possessed). The power of extracting salutary qualities from Evil itself, also finds a place:

> O filthy grandeur! sublime ignominy!

With Love, as with Beauty, good predominates over Evil. But Baudelaire's unwavering lucidity refused to minimize the importance of sin, which, in his eyes, was inseparable from physical love. His attitude on this question could be discovered from the assertion in *Fusées:* "As for myself, I say: the unique, the supreme delight of love lies in the certainty of doing evil."

In contrast to this form of love, we next come upon the cycle named after Madame Sabatier, which can be called the "Cycle of Spiritual Love." Madame Sabatier received the first anonymous tributes from Baudelaire in 1852. This date marked Baudelaire's open break with *l'École païenne,* a time when his works do not conceal his abounding spirituality. This state of idealistic exaltation may have led him to a Platonic attachment. In the first poem he addressed to Madame Sabatier, on December 9, "À celle qui est trop gaie" (To One Who Is Too Gay), he contrasted her innocence to his guilt by means of unusual and cruel imagery. In "Réversibilité" (Reversibility), apparently his second poem to her, she was elevated to an angelic position, and was held up as a creature exempt from all human baseness. Her admirer, excluding any possibility of an ordinary physical liaison with her, did not plead for anything more than her intercession:

> Angel of happiness, of joy, and of light,
> David, dying, would have sought health again
> In the fragrance of your enchanted body;
> But I myself ask only prayers of you,
> Angel of happiness, of joy, and of light.

All the other poems of this cycle make the same plea "to the angel and immortal goddess," who possesses the purifying and elevating properties of an "Aube spirituelle" (Spiritual Dawn):

> I am your guardian Angel, your Muse, your Madonna!

In only one poem, "Confession," does he depart from this purity and expose the torment which it conceals. "Once, only once . . ." We can interpret this poem as Baudelaire's involuntary avowal of the true meaning of his Platonic sentiments. It is difficult to imagine that such a lucid mind was capable of self-delusion about this good and beautiful woman, whose "spiritual flesh," as he well knew, was familiar with all physical weaknesses. It is likely that he saw in her his ideal of perfect love, that is, love free from the curse of sin. Only an "incorruptible love" could help him

> Pour into his thirsty soul
> The taste of the eternal.

Perhaps we should not completely ignore the rather quaint theories of Enfantin and Flora Tristan, according to whom women, acting somewhat like intermediary agents, play the role of Messiahs. Though he was generally suspicious of heresies of any kind, Baudelaire had dabbled at one time in such obscure mystical doctrines as the one we have just described. He might have cast Madame Sabatier in such a role. Certain passages of his letters seem to suggest it: "As a final remark, in order to explain my moments of silence and my moments of intensity, an intensity which is almost religious, I will tell you that when my being is engulfed in its night of depravity and innate foolishness, it muses deeply on you. This provocative and purifying meditation gives rise to a fortunate development. . . . My egotism prompts me to take advantage of you." These statements were only made under the cover of anonymity. Even when he terminated their relationship in 1857, he expressed his feelings in rather cool tones: "Imagine a fusion of sympathy, respect, and longing, along with large doses of childish foolishness, full of earnestness, and you will arrive at an approximation of that indefinable something which I feel sincerely but find myself incapable of expressing more perfectly. . . . You are more than my beloved and cherished dream, you are my superstition."

All the eccentricities of this story become understandable if we realize that Baudelaire's love was consciously built around an ideal image which he found embodied in the person of Madame Sabatier. We are thus able to comprehend his complete lack of jealousy toward Mosselman, the banker and "protector" of this "sweet and lovable woman," as well as his reluctance to reveal himself as the author of the epistles. This was also the reason for the disastrous outcome of the beautiful Madame Sabatier's simple offer: an offer which had not usually engendered complications. In the letter announcing his break, which so completely disconcerted his correspondent, Baudelaire did not even attempt to disguise his refusal. "And lastly, lastly, a few days ago you were a divinity, which was so nice, so charming, and so sacred. Now you are a woman." Clearly, his hymns of worship were not addressed to the woman.

This affair only affects our curiosity. But it was necessary for us to examine it, in order to define the features of this second cycle of love poems. Perhaps the cycle named after Marie Daubrun constitutes another group of love poems, but this is open to question. This cycle does not represent a definite *type* of love, as do the two preceding ones. From a chronological point of view, the affair with Marie Daubrun seems to have come before the one with Madame Sabatier. But actually we are very poorly informed on the subject. Our sole piece of evidence is Baudelaire's one rather mysterious and undated letter, bearing an address which does not appear on any of his other letters, and mentioning merely the first name of the addressee. The identification of this Marie as the beautiful actress who rose to fame through her role in *La Belle aux cheveux d'or* (The Girl with Golden Hair) seems very probable though not certain. The story of her relations with Baudelaire also remains in the realm of conjecture. Certain indications and cross-checkings allow us to theorize that their connection took place in 1846 or 1847. It is known that Marie Daubrun was Banville's mistress between 1855 and 1860, and inspired several of his verses. Some biographers even suppose that she was the reason for the break between the two poets. But we have no evidence of such an occurrence.

The letter addressed to "Marie" informs us that the actress had rejected Baudelaire's advances, and the latter, having easily resigned himself to the situation, merely expressed sentiments very similar to those he was soon to feel for Madame Sabatier. "That I am in love with you, Marie, I cannot deny; but the love that I bear towards you is that of a Christian for his God; neither should you ever give so common and shameful a name to this incorporeal and mysterious devotion, to this chaste and delicate attraction, which draws my soul to yours, in spite of your wishes. . . . Henceforward you will be my only queen, my passion, and my beauty; you are that part of my being which has been formed by a spiritual essence. . . . Be my Angel, my Muse, and my Madonna, and lead me in the path of Beauty." One can recognize not only the spirit, but the very words which we later find in the poems dedicated to Madame Sabatier. Baudelaire's sentiments were based on his own need, and not on an attraction for any particular person.

Nevertheless, the poems do possess their own distinct quality. Some, as for instance "L'Invitation au voyage" (Invitation to a Journey), are comparable to certain passages of the letter. On the whole they express fatherly or brotherly affection, but they are not devoid of beguiling and penetrating sensuality. If we attempt to name this cycle, as we have named the two preceding ones, we could call it the "Cycle of Equivocal Love."

We have no reason to believe that all the poems included in this section (from XLIX to LVII in the second edition) were written for the same woman. We can only surmise that they were deliberately grouped together since they express analogous sentiments. But their tone is not uniform. After the placid mildness of "Le beau Navire" (The Splendid Ship) and "L'Invitation au voyage," the four concluding pieces are filled with a dark fury which reminds us of the earlier condemnations of physical love.

The next seven poems, dedicated to, and inspired by, isolated (and unidentified) women, all end on the same note as the "Sonnet d'automne" (Autumn Sonnet):

> Sinister in his watch-tower,
> Love waits in ambush, bending his fatal bow.
> I know the weapons of his ancient arsenal:
>
> Crime, horror, and madness.

This is followed by several fanciful or fantastic pieces. The first part is then terminated by a "splenetic" series: a tragic progression of powerful intensity. The last three poems form a conclusion in which Baudelaire summed up his conception of man. In the first edition, "L'Héautontimorouménos" was placed directly after the cycle of Marie Daubrun. Here in the second edition, it assumes its original purpose; it elaborates the second part of the epilogue which Baudelaire had intended to write in 1855. Its opening theme is that of the satisfaction obtained by inflicting suffering upon another in the course of a love affair. But it appears that this suffering ricochets back to the author:

> I am the wound and the knife!
> I am the slap and the cheek!
> I am the limbs and the rack:
> The victim and the executioner, both.

Actually, this is the human condition, which Baudelaire realized in his own person. "L'Irrémédiable" (The Irremediable) depicts, in an increasingly terrifying sequence, man caught in the web of his own vices by "his persistence in Evil perceived." All excuses, all remedies, are impossible. Finally, "L'Horloge" (The Clock) is a protest against that procrastination which caused him so much suffering and to which he ascribed Satanic origins. It is not the postponement of material plans that he denounced in this poem, but the breaking of good resolutions. Here again, Baudelaire borrowed his theme from the pulpit, concluding, in the same vein, not with a merciless condemnation, but with a solemn and threatening warning.

As we have seen, the denouement of "Spleen et Idéal" was greatly changed in the second edition. In conformity with the general plan of the work, the final poems deal exclusively with the artist. But the lengthy series of sixteen poems implicates all humanity and is concerned with salvation, rather than with a momentary escape from reality. The final poem offers the solution of immediate and thorough reform.

The "Tableaux parisiens" (Parisian Scenes), which constitute the second part of *Les Fleurs du Mal,* are the result of a new grouping which was not present in the 1857 edition. Ten out of eighteen of the poems are new. In spite of the title, we should not expect descriptive poems. Anatole France saw in Baudelaire a poet of the metropolis: "He sensed the workaday world of Paris; he sensed the charm of the suburbs. . . ." But these "scenes" were not painted by a mere observer. He encountered the same fundamental struggles of the human condition on every street and intersection. However, his technique had switched from introspection to exterior investigation, and though occasional poems in the first person are still to be found in the remainder of the volume, henceforth they will be written in the tone of a witness and not a subject.

The arrangement of the poems seems to be governed by various designs here: on the one hand, spectacles of the day and the night, of exteriors and interiors; on the other hand, meditations full of melancholy and compassion, alternating with "scenes" ablaze with the violence and horror of evil. The only three poems which are relatively optimistic are placed in the beginning, as hopes or illusions which will be easily shattered.

The ensuing part, "Le Vin," constitutes a natural continuation of the "Tableaux parisiens." It takes on a new meaning, withdrawing the idea of the efficiency originally allowed to intoxication as a means of escape.

The reader who comes upon these poems, halfway between the "Tableaux parisiens" and "Fleurs du Mal," can only view intoxication as a temporary relief, incapable of saving man from his sufferings. The five poems in this section seem to be early pieces. According to Prarond, three of them were composed before 1843. In any case, none of them were written after 1851, when Baudelaire published "Du Vin et du hachich" [*sic*] (Concerning Wine and Hashish). In that work, he used the same themes and sometimes even the identical words, but, anticipating the severe condemnation he later pronounced in *Paradis artificiels*, he passed unfavorable judgment on wine and intoxication. However, he made an explicit distinction between wine and hashish, seeing in the former "a physical consolation," while the latter constituted "moral support for suicide." His defense of wine is based in part on humanitarian considerations: "Wine is for the working class, who deserves to drink it." In the 1861 edition, drunkenness was considered from an objective, rather than a personal, point of view—in spite of "Le Vin du solitaire" (The Solitary Man's Wine)—and takes its place before "Les Fleurs du Mal" in the category of the lawless and condemnable efforts made by man to escape from the necessities of his condition.

This is the meaning we ascribe to the poems included under the title of "Fleurs du Mal." The scope of this title is more limited here than when it is applied to the work as a whole. From the very beginning, Baudelaire forcefully denounced the Satanic character of sensual delights.

> At my side, the Demon works ceaselessly;
> He swims around me like an impalpable ether;
> I breathe him in, he burns my lungs
> And fills me with desire, eternal and sinful.

Moreover, the following tercets uncover not only the deceptive charms of evil, but also its disastrous consequences:

> And so he leads me, far from the sight of God,
> Panting and broken with weariness, into the center
> Of the plains of Boredom, endless and deserted,
>
> And before my eyes, full of confusion, he hurls
> The sight of soiled clothes and of open wounds
> And all the bloody vestments of Destruction.

If Baudelaire was speaking for himself here, most of the poems which follow cannot be applied to him, though they unanimously confirm the views he had formulated about the temptations and consequences of sensuality. These views are consistent with those he expressed on other occasions, especially in his *Journaux intimes*.

"Révolte" raises a difficult question. Should we consider these three poems to be an expression of Baudelaire's personal revolt, they would refute the numerous passages we have previously quoted, wherein he expressed his religious faith in no uncertain terms. This is the opinion which is widely accepted. No one would think of seriously considering the notice which preceded this part in the first edition. It is looked upon as a precautionary measure, rhetorical and sarcastic at the same time. There is some truth in this opinion, but this is no reason to disregard the notice. If we cannot regard these poems as the calculated fabrications of a "perfect performer," or write off his "Le Reniement de saint Pierre" as a mere "pastiche," it would also be difficult to question the sincerity of the concluding sentences of the notice, which express sentiments typical of Baudelaire. His respect for "our Savior, Jesus Christ, the eternal and willing Victim" is made manifest each time he invokes the "glorious infant of Judea, the Sage of sages, the Word incarnate." As for the Pharisee's prayer, this was a motif he had used more than once, and he felt it to be of such grave consequence that he planned to make it the subject of one of his prose poems. It should be clear, therefore, that this notice was a mixture of sarcasm and sincerity. "Révolte" was conceived with the same intentions as "Tableaux parisiens," "Le Vin," and "Fleurs du Mal." It is a manifestation of Evil and of a Satanic disposition of which the author partakes, but which is not personal to him. He knew the temptations of revolt as well as those of sensuality—who does not? But it is unlikely that these three poems express the normal path of his thought.

"La Mort" concludes the volume. However, this was not its original place: a "final piece, or epilogue, addressed to the city of Paris" was to have been added. This epilogue, which Baudelaire had mentioned in a letter of 1860, was to have been made up of sonorous tercets, and was never finished. We do possess several fragments of it. They emphasize the relatively impersonal character of the work, which was the result of the change of perspective in the second edition, as we have already noted. The fate of the artist was replaced as a subject of reflection by the spiritual struggles taking place in the whole city.

Perhaps we should not regret that Baudelaire relinquished this projected epilogue. The theme of imprecation against the metropolis had already lost its originality. It had been treated by Vigny, Gautier, Lefèvre-Deumier, Lassailly, Barbier, Banville, and a few others. Moreover, to bring *Les Fleurs du Mal* to a conclusion circumscribed by the Parisian sky would have been to arbitrarily limit the scope of this book which, as it stands, takes on the dimensions of a universal drama.

The chapter entitled "La Mort" poses certain problems. In 1857 it was composed of three sonnets, the final tercets of which brought one to the gateway of a new Life "in unknown skies." Nothing could have been more in conformity with Baudelaire's spirituality. In 1861, these sonnets were followed by three other poems, the last two of which were also sonnets: "La Fin de la journée" (The End of the Day) and "Le Rêve d'un curieux" (Dream of a Curious Person). In "La Fin de la journée," death is welcomed as a soothing sleep:

> At last!
> My spirit, like my jaded spine,
> Pleads hungrily for rest.
> With my heart full of mournful dreams
>
> I shall lie on my back
> And roll myself in your curtains,
> O you refreshing shadows!

In contrast, "Le Rêve d'un curieux" expresses, as the title indicates, a keen curiosity:

> I was like a child, eager for the Show,
> Hating the curtain as one hates an obstacle.

This curiosity was strangely frustrated:

> The curtain was lifted, and I was still waiting.

This poem, however, does not express disbelief in the "wonders awaiting us beyond the grave." No doubt, Baudelaire's faith knew many weak moments, but in spite of his doubts it does not seem likely that he would have ended this work with a plain and simple negation. This sonnet embodies the dream of a believer:

> Anguish, and living hope, without dissent . . .

This poem could have been a reference to a specific nightmare, with no other purpose than to portray the void which the absence of God would create in us. Or, it could be an expression of the anguished doubt, which Baudelaire had already experienced and voiced in the poems of the "Fleurs du Mal" or "Révolte."

The final piece of the volume, the poem "Le Voyage," is also the longest. It had not been planned for the conclusion: its composition had preceded that of the projected epilogue. But it makes an appropriate ending, since it combines and evaluates the themes developed in the entire work:

Everywhere, without seeking it out, we have seen,
From the top to the bottom of the fatal scale,
The boring spectacle of immortal sin.

If this voyage merely provokes our disgust and results in all kinds of failure, if our own image reflected by the world reveals only

An oasis of horror in a desert of boredom

how can we picture death, if not as a deliverance desired at any cost, no matter what fate awaits us in the beyond?

This final poem does not invalidate our hypothesis about *Les Fleurs du Mal*. It does not imply indifference to salvation, a source of permanent anxiety for Baudelaire, but it expresses man's despondency and weariness in the face of his incapacity to elevate his life to the level of his dreams. This is a cruel balance-sheet, but one which, in its very hopelessness, gives evidence of the uncompromising demands made by the poet.

10 · *Evocative Sorcery*

THE DISTINCTION between matter and form is no longer an issue. Nevertheless, we adopt a different point of view for prose and for poetry. In prose the form should be subordinate to the content; the opposite should be true of poetry. If we should accept Valéry's explications, the subject of his poetry would be of no consequence. It was determined by the form. This was also Edgar Allan Poe's theory in his "Philosophy of Composition." But in his "Poetic Principle" he denied this idea, and we know Baudelaire's opinion about it.

Baudelaire had always attached much importance to content in both his literary and art criticism: "In addition to the love which must impregnate the humblest work of art, I believe that the subject matter contributes to the genius of the artist," he stated in his *Salon de 1859*. Seldom have the aesthetic principles of a work of literature been so intimately fused with the content as in *Les Fleurs du Mal*. Could one even speak of content, in the accepted sense of the word? It is impossible to separate it, not only from the form of these poems, but from Baudelaire's very idea of poetry. We refer the reader to Baudelaire's definition of poetry which he formulated in connection with Romanticism, and to the one in his "Notes nouvelles sur Edgar Poe," which he quoted once more in his Notice of 1859 on Théophile Gautier, when he wrote that the emotion produced by an "exquisite poem" "gives evidence of an aggravated melancholy and strained nerves, of a nature banished to an imperfect world, but desirous of immediate access to paradise while still within the confines of this world." Is not *Les Fleurs du Mal* the exact expression "of a nature banished to an imperfect world, but desirous of immediate access to paradise while still within the confines of this world"? A better definition of this book could not be found. Baudelaire had created an identity between the subject matter of his masterpiece and the function he assigned to poetry.

A poem, in order to attain its object, should communicate this emotion, or "aggravated melancholy," to the reader. In Baudelaire's own words, the employment of "all the means at the disposal of the arts" would not be excessive for the realization of this goal. What are these "means" which he never specified, but which he boasted of possessing and mastering completely, and which he facetiously offered to teach in "twenty lessons"? We must assume that these are not the ordinary techniques of verse, for their application has for a long time baffled public and critics alike. The critics have not only reproached him for his macabre and sickening tastes, but have charged him with incompetent craftsmanship. "It would be difficult to find verses which are more belabored or longwinded than his," wrote Brunetière. In his *Versification et métrique de Baudelaire* (Poetics and Meters of Baudelaire), Albert Cassagne aptly observed that if one were to judge Baudelaire by the principles set forth by Maurice Grammont, one would classify him among the least harmonious of the poets. Many have condemned his prosaic style, his clumsiness, his meagre inspiration, and his scanty imagery.

And indeed, we do come upon many awkward phrases and stylistic imperfections in these poems, many disconcerting repetitions. "Parfum exotique" and "La Chevelure," which follow each other, contain not only identical combinations of rhymes, *climats* and *mâts*, but also two very similar lines of expression:

> *Je vois un port rempli de* voiles *et de* mâts . . .
>
> (I see a harbor full of *sails* and *masts* . . .)

in one, and:

> . . . *un éblouissant rêve*
> *De* voiles, *de rameurs, de flammes et de* mâts . . .
>
> (. . . a dazzling dream
> Of *sails*, of oarsmen, of flames, and of *masts* . . .)

in the other. In other instances, the author unhesitatingly used the same expressions: "your heavy mane," for example, turns up in both "La Chevelure" and "Le Léthé" (Lethe), and "missing palm trees" in "Le Cygne" (The Swan) and "A une Malabaraise." At times, repetitions even occur in the same stanza:

—Soyez béni, mon Dieu, qui donnez la souffrance
Comme un divin remède a nos impuretés
Et comme la meilleure et la plus pure *essence. . . .*

(Be blessed, my God, who gives suffering
As a divine cure for our *impurity,*
And as the best and *purest* essence. . . .)

Je veux te raconter, ô molle enchanteresse!
Les diverses beautés *qui parent ta jeunesse;*
Je veux te peindre ta beauté. . . .

(I want to list for you, oh sweet enchantress,
The diverse *beauties* which set off your youth.
I want to paint your *beauty* for you. . . .)

And not much farther we find:

. . . *Ouvrent leurs vastes* bras *pour* embrasser *la gloire* . . .

(Their vast arms open to encompass Glory . . .)

This last is an excusable metaphor, though not a very successful one, especially since the "bras" (arms) were those of vessels. We should note that these examples have been taken from poems which are deemed to be among Baudelaire's most beautiful.

The entire work abounds in trivialities. One notices such words and phrases as: *stink and stench, to baulk, to yelp, to twist, to strut, to be entangled, to have a tussle, filth, carrion, idiotic, to cringe, bungler, dwarfish, being low on money, making the bum split his sides with laughter,* etc. Awkward and prosaic verses, as well as weak lines, turn up even in his most celebrated poems. The first three stanzas of "L'Albatros" are mediocre, and the second stanza of "Recueillement" (Meditation) is inferior to the rest, as Valéry has pointed out.

But was he right in reproaching Baudelaire? The question is not as simple as it seems. Let us recall, first of all, that Baudelaire continually made a distinction in his critical writings on art between the beauty in a work of art and the perfection of its technique. He even declared "that there is a great difference between a *completed* work and one that is *finished;* that in general that which is *completed* is not *finished,* and that an extremely *finished* work could very well not be *complete* at all; that the value of a clever stroke, appropriately placed and predominant, is enormous." He also emphasized continually the importance of subordinating detail to the work as a whole: a privilege of genius, and a quality which he hailed in Delacroix. "Forever sacrificing the detail to the ensemble, and fearing to weaken the vitality of his inspiration in the weariness brought about by a more precise and calligraphic execution, Delacroix possesses an indefinable originality which comes from close association with his subject." It is quite out of the question to deny the imperfections of his poetry, which are consistent with his style. Some of them are not real imperfections and are only considered as such by misappreciation of his art's true originality.

As for the "weakness" of certain lines and stanzas, we have the clarification that Baudelaire himself seems to have made, through the pen of his friend Asselineau. Asselineau wrote the preface to "La double Vie" (The Double Life), a collection of short stories published by Poulet-Malassis in 1858. Baudelaire had written a very favorable article about the work. He had personally annotated the preface. After having studied the text and the comments, Jacques Crépet came to the conclusion that he had actually inspired it; this is why he ascribed such importance to it. It contains a passage which is, in all probability, an account of a conversation between Baudelaire and Calonne. "I overheard, in a printer's office, the following exchange between the director of one of the most reputable reviews and a noted poet: 'Don't you think, Sir, that this line is a bit weak?' 'Yes, Sir,' replied the poet, biting his lips, 'and the following line is weak also, but they are there to lead up to the next one, which is not weak at all.' 'I will not deny that, Sir, but it would be infinitely preferable if the three of them were of equal force.' 'No, Sir,' replied the poet, angrily this time. 'For then what would happen to the gradation? This is an art, Sir, an art that has taken me twenty years to learn, and . . .'—he did not dare to add: 'about which you do not know the first thing.' "

This is a lesson we should keep in mind while appraising

Baudelaire's work. We know what his goals were in the realm of poetry. Our task is to decide if he attained them. In regard to this, let us repeat a statement he made concerning his beloved Delacroix: "What is the use of pointing out insignificant mistakes and microscopic blemishes? The ensemble is breathtaking."

Baudelaire did not scorn to use traditional means, even those which were not in the best standing among refined intellectuals, for instance, the methods of rhetoric. He has been blamed for such usage, but he, on the other hand, congratulated himself for it: "If a rhetor I must be, then a rhetor I am, and will be proud of being." This was not just a quip, made in an off-hand manner; on several occasions he declared his propensity for the art of rhetoric which, after all, is nothing else than the art of style. If one concedes the existence of this art, one must also admit that it has its own techniques, and even its own laws. No writer can do without it. Rhetoric is not in conflict with the natural order of things, but consciously makes use of the natural order. As long as its use is in conformity with the subject, it is justifiable. When a subject is weighty, noble, or moving, one cannot help using expressions of solemnity, nobility, and pathos. Instead of wrestling with such requirements, Baudelaire dived in without hesitation, with all his genius and all his sincerity. To single out some characteristic examples, we mention first the sequence of nine exclamatory lines in "J'aime le souvenir de ces époques nues . . ." and the last stanzas of the two poems entitled "Femmes damnées" (Damned Women), especially that of "Delphine et Hippolyte":

> Descend, descend, you piteous victims . . .

In these instances, moral judgment provokes the change of tone and imposes an oratorical manner. This is also the case in the second quatrain of "Recueillement," which offended Valéry's sensibilities. This moral judgment, which was indispensable to Baudelaire's poetic theories, could not have been conveyed so effectively in less rhetorical tones.

Another means of expression, which bears a relationship to rhetoric and which Baudelaire frequently employed is allegory: "this genre which is so spiritual that clumsy painters have accustomed us to look upon it with suspicion. Allegory is actually one of the most ancient and most natural forms of poetry."

The pictures, engravings, and pieces of sculpture which Baudelaire had used as motifs in *Les Fleurs du Mal* are allegorical. These occur in the poem entitled "Allégorie," and in "Le Masque," "Une Gravure fantastique" (A Fantastic Engraving), "Le Squelette laboureur" (The Digging Skeleton), "Danse macabre" (The Dance of Death), "Une Martyre" (A Martyr), and "L'Amour et la crâne." Plastic representation seldom resulted in poetic inspiration for him unless he could give it an allegorial interpretation, as in his sonnet entitled, "Sur *Le Tasse en prison*" (On Eugene Delacroix's Picture of *Tasso in Prison*). In these instances the word "allegorical" is used in its loosest sense, as when we use it to describe such poems as "L'Albatros," "La Muse malade" (The Sick Muse) and "La Muse vénale" (The Venal Muse), "Le Beau Navire," "L'Horloge," "Le Cygne," and many others. Even in the strict sense, many allegories can be found in *Les Fleurs du Mal*. They include not only the common varieties of Time, Love, Beauty, Death, and Chance, but also Hope, Anguish, Irony, Pleasure, Virtue, Repentance, Work, Devotion, Folly, Madness, and Debauchery and Death—those "two gracious sisters"—and, in the scope of a single sonnet, Sorrow, Pleasure, the Years, Regret, and Night. Nothingness itself is personified! Rightfully did Baudelaire claim in "Le Cygne":

. . . for me, everything becomes allegory.

As we have seen, he did not make the mistake of drawing only from the traditional stockpile of poetic expression; he did, however, include the accepted formulas of verse-making. It would be wearisome to make a complete survey of his use of alliteration and consonance. Here are a few striking examples:

Durant les noirs *ennuis des* neigeuses *soirées* . . .

Et mes yeux dans le noir *devinaient tes prunelles* . . .

Et cognent en volant les volets et l'auvent . . .

Quand la pierre, *opprimant ta* poitrine peureuse . . .

and this particularly successful consonance:

Les houles, *en* roulant *les images des cieux* . . .

Baudelaire made free use of these techniques, which have always been familiar to poets endowed with a penchant for musical language. If he distinguished himself from his predecessors in this field it was through the quality of his music rather than the quantity of his effects. They were subtle. They did not stand out as forced contrivances bargaining for the reader's attention, as sometimes happens even in the poetry of Mallarmé or Valéry. They blend harmoniously into the substance of the poem and completely justify their presence.

Baudelaire also distinguished himself in the construction of rhythms and rhymes. He was not a great innovator of new rhythms. He used alexandrines and quatrains of alternating rhymes most frequently, even in his sonnets. The only poem which embodies a rhythm of his own invention with outstanding success is "L'Invitation au voyage," with its stanzas of twelve lines and couplets of refrain. The lines of five or seven syllables are arranged in subtle combinations and beautifully accentuated by the use of masculine and feminine rhymes.

Aside from this example his versification is not original, except for a few details which disclose an audacious and inventive mind. There are about ten poems in quatrains of alternating masculine and feminine rhymes. The quatrain of alternating masculine and feminine rhymes achieves an effect of absolute simplicity, but it demanded considerable control if Baudelaire was to avoid monotony. This technique helps to bewitch the reader when it is perfectly executed. We may perhaps venture to ascribe it to the influence of Marceline Desbordes-Valmore's poetry, which Baudelaire had read "with the eyes of youth, which, if they belong to sensitive persons, are intense and perspicacious at the same time." Baudelaire had a special regard for her, "probably because he finds himself so diametrically opposed to her." Verlaine was also indebted to this writer for his languorous couplets, which achieve effects similar to Baudelaire's.

Did Baudelaire borrow the technique of repetition from the same author? He had come across it more than once in her poetry, as, for instance, in "Son retour" (His Return):

> Alas! I should hate him!
> He has brought back sickness to my soul,
> This sickness full of tears and of flame,

So sorrowful, so slow to heal!
Alas! I should hate him.

In this case, it is the influence of Edgar Allan Poe which usually receives most of the credit. Certainly, Poe's work contains effects which are more related to those of Baudelaire than does the work of the French poetess. But it would be an oversimplification to see here only the influence of the American writer. Cassagne observed that poetic repetition was already present in "Les Yeux de Berthe" (Bertha's Eyes), which was probably composed prior to 1843. "Lesbos," the poem in which this technique was most abundantly used, appeared in 1851, before Baudelaire was acquainted with the poetry of Edgar Allan Poe. The American certainly encouraged him along this path, as he did on other occasions. But it is likely that Baudelaire had already acquired this technique either from Marceline Desbordes-Valmore, or directly from popular songs, especially those written by his friend, Pierre Dupont. The function Baudelaire assigned to repetition was essentially more poetic and musical than either of these writers. In this he resembled Edgar Allan Poe, but this was more of a coincidence than an influence.

Another sign of his independent attitude toward traditional versification is his unusually free handling of the sonnet form. He himself had related that Théophile Gautier had criticized the volume of verse put out by the Norman School for its immoderate use of "*free* sonnets . . . which gladly break away from the rule of quadruple rhymes." This criticism could certainly have been lodged against *Les Fleurs du Mal*, for Baudelaire had permitted himself the most fanciful combinations. The rhymes in his sonnets are arranged in all ways imaginable, in the quatrains as well as in the tercets. Out of a total of seventy sonnets—for he frequently employed this poetic form, from which he managed to extract most varied and powerful effects—only four strictly follow the regular patterns. He obtained still more daring results by varying the length of the lines: in "Le Chat" he alternated decasyllables with octosyllables, in "La Musique," alexandrines with lines of five syllables. Another technique he employed was to change the sequence of the stanzas: "Bien loin d'ici" is an inverted sonnet, and "L'Avertisseur" (The Serpent's Tooth) encloses the tercets between two quatrains. We conclude this list of literary curiosities by adding that Baudelaire was one of the first, along with Asselineau and Banville, to attempt to adapt the Malayan *pantoum* to French modes of versification. He did this in "Harmonie du soir" (Evening Harmony), which was certainly far removed from the oriental pattern, but possesses matchless poetic qualities.

The only revolutionary innovation which Baudelaire made in the field of versification was his total suppression of the auditive caesura in certain lines. This is perhaps the first instance of a systematic rebellion against the ancient precepts of Malherbe and Boileau. Victor Hugo had already considerably increased the proportion of ternary lines, but he remained within conventional bounds by keeping the caesura as an accented syllable. He assigned the same function to this interior enjambment as to actual runover lines by imposing a slight pause in spite of the requirements of sense and syntax:

Car ces derniers soldats/de la dernière guerre
Furent grands; ils avaient/vaincu toute la terre,
Chassé vingt rois, passé/les Alpes et le Rhin . . .

In contrast with Hugo's method, Baudelaire succeeded in completely eliminating the caesura. In his verse, the pause becomes impossible since it would isolate an article, a possessive or relative pronoun, a preposition, or a conjunction:

A la très-bonne, à la très/-belle, à la très-chère . . .

Il fait surgir plus d'un/portique fabuleux . . .

Je te ferai de mon/respect de beaux souliers

Tes nobles jambes, sous/les volants qu'elles chassent

Dans quel philtre, dans quel/vin, dans quelle tisane . . .

J'ai peur du sommeil comme/on a peur d'un grand trou . . .

The fact that one finds no less than about fifteen such lines in *Les Fleurs du Mal* points up their function. Baudelaire established total rhythmic liberty within the space of twelve syllables. Verlaine advanced only half a step more when he wrote this line in 1868, which was to provoke a smile on the youthful face of the adolescent Rimbaud, reading in Charleville:

Et la tigresse épouvantable d'Hyrcanie . . .

(And the terrifying tigress of Hyrcania . . .)

Verlaine granted himself the same freedom to use runover lines as Baudelaire had, in the course of his development of Baudelaire's innovation.

These features of Baudelaire's versification are not mere trifling details worthy of only the specialist's attention. First of all, the artist's techniques are always governed by what Baudelaire termed his "temperament" and correspond, therefore, to the fundamental conditions of his genius. The effect that Baudelaire achieved by this variety of techniques was one of unexpectedness. For him "irregularity, that is to say, the unexpected, the surprising, and the astonishing, are essential characteristics of beauty." This idea was deeply rooted in Baudelaire's mind. His *Salon de 1845* had concluded with this request: "May those who have the true spirit of adventure give us the singular joy of celebrating, in the coming year, the advent of something *new*!" His acquaintance with Edgar Allan Poe contributed to his interest in surprise, and to its integration with his other aesthetic principles. It was in his "Exposition universelle" that he fully expressed his ideas on the subject for the first time: "Astonishment constitutes one of the greatest pleasures of art and literature, . . ." and further, "Beauty is always bizarre." That was written a few months after his translation of *Ligéia* had appeared in print where the American author quoted Bacon's aphorism: "Exquisite beauty is inconceivable . . . without a certain *strangeness* in the proportions." In the course of attempts later made to explain this theory, it has been interpreted as a "minor form of masochism." This was not the explanation provided by Edgar Allan Poe in his *Marginalia,* which Baudelaire had carefully read: "Minus this element of strangeness . . . we lost all the existing beauties of the earth which enable us to dream of the beauties of Heaven." Compare this text with those already quoted wherein Baudelaire defined the function of poetry, and the fundamental role played by the element of surprise in his aesthetic system becomes apparent. Naturally, surprise does not exist for its own sake. After having stated that "Beauty is always bizarre," Baudelaire dispelled all possibilities of misinterpretation: "I do not mean to say that Beauty is deliberately, coldly bizarre, for in that case it would be a monster that has escaped from the confines of life. I mean that Beauty always contains a certain amount of strangeness, naïve strangeness, unforced and unconscious, and that it is this strangeness that stamps it as the Beautiful."

"Unforced," "unconscious": in Baudelaire's own work, everything was perfectly conscious and deliberate. But it is true that the strangeness, or, more simply, the surprise, are never gratuitous, conforming as they do to the particular nature of each poem. Let us refer to the examples we have previously cited, the most significant of them being the pantoum, "Harmonie du soir," which gives an indication of the astonishing use Baudelaire made of these "irregularities."

The use of surprise becomes more evident when we examine Baudelaire's language, imagery, and rhymes. The principal function of surprise is that of emphasizing and increasing the evocative power of words. The term "surprise" is not even quite suitable on all occasions, for the effect can often be described rather as an explosion or shock. Baudelaire was especially adept at onslaughts.

> You, who entered my plaintive heart
> Like the blow of a knife . . .
> Here is the charming evening, friend of the criminal . . .
>
> Be wise, oh my Sorrow . . .

The opening line of "Le Cygne" is set off like a firecracker, and explodes in our imaginations like a shower of stars:

> Andromache, I am thinking of you!

These examples bring us to the famous formula to be found in *Fusées*: "Language and composition, viewed as an operation of magic and evocative enchantment." Here again, we encounter an idea of long standing. As early as 1846, Baudelaire had rebuked his former schoolfellow, Louis Ménard. In a rather sarcastic article concerning *Prométhée délivré,* he said: "He does not know the meaning of powerfully rendered rhymes, the signposts which guide us along the path of ideas; he is likewise unaware of the effects one can achieve from a given number of words combined in various ways." He had already arrived at a rough idea of "evocative sorcery."

But when we arrive at the most original novelty inaugurated by Baudelaire there are no rules nor visible signs. In a draft of the preface for *Les Fleurs du Mal*, he assures us: "That French poetry possesses a mysterious and unrecognized prosody, like the Latin and English languages . . .

"That the poetic phrase can imitate (and in this, poetry is like the art of music and the science of mathematics) a horizontal line, or an ascending or descending vertical line. It can rise straight up to heaven without losing its breath, or fall straight down to hell with the velocity of any weight. It can follow a spiral, describe a parabola, or a zigzag line, making a series of superimposed angles;

"That poetry is like the arts of painting, cooking, and cosmetics in its ability to express every sensation of sweetness or bitterness, of beatitude or horror, by pairing a certain noun with a certain adjective, in analogy or contrast."

He offered to teach this art in twenty lessons. It might have proved interesting to have put him to the test. He had clearly indicated the possible effects, but had not defined the means. Perhaps there is nothing to define, and we must limit ourselves to noting the effects whenever we happen to encounter them. But it would not be fruitless for us to devote a cursory glance of consideration to this "sorcery." Baudelaire's conception of poetry at this point has gone beyond the possibilities offered by versification. He was hardly the person to neglect versification as such, but the way in which he made use of the traditional modes shows that he was not intent on exploiting them completely, in the manner of a Ronsard or a Hugo. He employed them as a base from which to explore new territories. Versification served as his springboard.

This springboard was indispensable. However, we cannot probe the originality of his poetry through metrical analysis or through a study of his techniques as a versemaker. Here he differed from his predecessors only by the audacity of his experiments and his subtle musicality. This difference is, of course, very important. But Baudelaire's essentially new quality consisted in the direct exploitation of the internal poetic resources of language. Certainly, no genuine poet can be unaware of the evocative power of words, but Baudelaire was the first to exploit this power so completely. His genius accomplished this task so successfully that none who followed in his tracks ever matched the wealth and variety of his poetry, no matter how great their talents. There is nothing more intriguing than those "effects one can gain from a given number of words combined in various ways."

We have no general principles, no practical rules, and no precepts to guide us in the matter. The most we can do is to make a minute analysis of the combined words of a given line and propose a possibly valid explanation applicable to that single instance.

This does not preclude the possibility of pointing out a few of the elements of Baudelairean poetry which give it its unique timbre. If we grant that words are endowed with a given weight, or with a certain range of meaning, then by timbre we mean the interaction of these various ranges of meaning, just as the timbre of an orchestra is made up of the network of sounds produced by the instruments. Before studying the combinations of particular words, it is necessary to examine the peculiarities of the vocabulary. A task of this magnitude would exceed the scope of this study. We can only indicate some of the extraordinary features which seem to dominate this symphony, which is both subtle and powerful.

We point out, in passing, the use of words which describe scents. Perhaps it would be preferable to use, as Baudelaire has done on more than one occasion, the term "smell" or "fragrance" rather than "scent," since olfactory sensations are extremely varied. They share common characteristics, however: they are bewildering and penetrating. (There are, of course, even in Baudelaire's poetry, a few exceptions: "the fragrance of youth," "the balm of angels," etc.) The gamut of scents includes nard, incense, myrrh, amber, musk, benjamin gum, olibanum, and many others: coconut oil, tar, fur, "savage and bestial scents," "acrid odors," "exhalations," and "emanations." Our sense of smell is overwhelmed in almost every poem. Baudelaire's entire work is permeated with scents.

Words evoking light and minerals convey another range of sensations:

> This earth, glowing with metal and stone,
> Fills me with ecstacy, and I love almost to madness
> Those things in which sound melts into light.

He employed them according to their immediate meanings, often as the components of some of the most startling images:

> Of pleasures more acute than ice or fire . . .

Brightness and hardness, on one hand, and scents and smells, on the other, belong to completely different and unrelated compartments of reality. Their association invests them with striking qualities.

In order to pursue our analysis, let us isolate another element: the use of abstract words, words which have generally been avoided by poets. Baudelaire often placed one of them deliberately at the end of one line, thereby duplicating its value. Though he often availed himself of the simpler words, such as beauty, brightness, pride, and pleasure, he did not shun the longer and less malleable ones: humanity, eternity, fraternity, insanity, capability, immortality, and incuriosity, thus obtaining unusual effects. Religious and theological terminology also occupies a prominent position, sometimes in its own context, and sometimes as a means of expressing love. Baudelaire had sternly rebuked other poets for this "sickening impiety." "They might just as well smear an altar with their excrement." To exonerate him, we must point out that this religious vocabulary is hardly out of the cycle of Madame Sabatier, the "Cycle of Spiritual Love." As for the poem "À une Madone" (To a Madonna), we cannot include it in this accusation, since it is entirely allegorical.

This brings us to what we have previously said about the abundance of allegory in *Les Fleurs du Mal.* There is an obvious connection between allegory, abstraction, and religious vocabulary. Words of this type evoke a kind of spirituality, and lend a very special atmosphere to the poems in which they are used.

In order to complete this brief review of Baudelaire's work, we must take up once again the charge of vulgarity which has been made against him. Far from being a defect, vulgarity in Baudelaire's poetry is artfully calculated to produce effects which are violent, contrasting, or unforeseen. (The exceptions are those few instances when the vulgar term was chosen simply for its expressive value.) This mixture of vulgarity with the most dignified kind of poetry was not only the result of Baudelaire's unusual temperament, but also grew out of the examples furnished by poets of the time of Henry IV and Louis XIII, especially Agrippa d'Aubigne. The following lines are reminiscent of these earlier writers:

> Each day we travel step by step towards Hell,
> Crossing, without horror, a darkness which *stinks.*

Vulgarity can also be a means of anchoring poetry to immediate reality, and of preventing it from losing itself in the "ethereal regions" where it has a habit of straying.

Lastly, among the prevailing timbres of the complex harmony we have tried to analyze, we discern still another quality, less apparent, and delicately fused with the whole: a cat-like quality, a kind of furry softness under which one can almost feel the claws. This disquieting sleekness, pregnant with hidden meanings, is sometimes evoked by the unexpected caress of an expressive "my dear," "my love," "my dark beauty," and at other times by a barely perceptible, and yet perceived, inflection. A most obvious and significant example is provided by the first stanza of "Une Charogne," where even the rhyme is charged with paradox:

> *Rappelez-vous l'objet que nous vîmes,* mon âme,
> *Ce beau matin d'été si doux:*
> *Au détour d'un sentier* une charogne infâme
> *Sur un lit semé de cailloux . . .*

> Do you remember the thing that we saw, *my soul,*
> On that beautiful summering morning
> At the turn of a path: *a hideous carrion*
> On a bed strewn with pebbles . . .

Rhyme was one of the poetic devices that Baudelaire worked out most carefully. It bears all the emphasis and weight of the line. If Louis Ménard ignored the effects of "powerfully rendered rhymes, these signposts which guide us along the path of ideas," as Baudelaire calls them, he himself was acquainted with all their secrets. He was aware of the poetic resonance of a proper noun full of evocative power. At the end of his lines we find the names of many places: from the Loire to the Ganges, from Africa to China, from the Capitol to the Carousel, from Siberia to the Sahara, from Icaria to the Americas, from Cythera to Palmyra, from Capua to Leucatia. We also find a complete mythology embracing Venus, Proserpine, Charon, the Danaides, Lethe, and the Hydra of Lerne. Legend, history, poets, and artists all contribute to the enrichment of the rhyme. The same goes for uncommon terms, which are used rather sparsely in *Les Fleurs du Mal,* but which almost always occupy this place of honor: trismegist, helminths, brach, hookah, gouge, scow, calenture, snow-leopard, water-sprite, dittany; and unusual rhymes, such as *alambic* and *aspic, aiguë,* and *ciguë,* the four rhymes ending in *urnes* in "La Muse malade," and the four rhymes ending in *avane*—unique in the French language—in "Sed non satiata" (But Not Satisfied); *couvercle* and *cercle,* also the only examples of this ending. Baudelaire was also fond of Latin phrases: *Te Deum, De profundis, Esto memor,* etc. He did not neglect the phonetic possibilities of rhyme any more than the other exterior elements of prosody.

A thorough study of his imagery would also yield extremely interesting results, but is not within the scope of this book. Jules Laforgue was struck by the unexpected nature of some of Baudelaire's images: "these fresh-hewn comparisons which casually but suddenly catch us unawares amidst the harmonious placidity of a line." And indeed, there are some of an astounding originality:

> Your triumphant throat is a beautiful armoire . . .
>
> Like a sob cut short by a spurt of blood,
> The cry of a rooster rends the hazy air . . .

When the effect produced is merely that of surprise, we can refer to the aesthetic principle which we have previously set forth. Much of this imagery, whether surprising or not, contains a common characteristic: it brings us back to man. While most poets turn to nature as the source of their imagery, Baudelaire quite often followed the opposite procedure:

> Great woods, you frighten me, *like cathedrals* . . .
>
> Each flower gives forth scent, *like an incense burner* . . .
>
> When the low and heavy sky weighs on us *like a lid* . . .

In fact, he rarely used nature as his starting-point, but the abstract idea in itself often called for human parallels, sometimes through unforeseen detours:

> Intangible Pleasure will flee towards the horizon
> Like a sylph running behind the stage . . .

Human creations lead to other human creations:

> The chimneys, the clock-towers, *these masts of the city* . . .

By these means he achieved his effects of surprise, and kept the attention and imagination of the reader rooted to the heart of his subject.

If this cursory glance has helped us to distinguish the basic elements of Baudelaire's tonality, it has not given us an idea of the orchestration by which he carried out the recommendations set forth in the draft of his preface: "imitate a horizontal line, an ascending or descending vertical line, follow a spiral, describe a parabola or a zigzag line, making a series of superimposed angles . . . express all sensations of sweetness or bitterness, of beatitude or horror, by pairing a certain adjective with a certain noun, in analogy or contrast." Sonnets such as "La Vie antérieure" and "Parfum exotique" constitute unparalleled achievements in this respect, due to their flawless internal and external harmony and to the almost vertiginous intensity of their magic. But his most striking achievement is probably to have been able to conjure up echoes with strains of the flute and the harp, as in *Tristesses de la lune,* as well as those "strange fanfares" which clang with the crash of cymbals and brass, as in *L'Irréparable:*

> Can we suffocate the old, the long Remorse
> Which lives, and thrives, and twists itself around,
> And feeds on us as the worm on the dead,
> As the caterpillar on the oak?
> Can we suffocate implacable Remorse?

In what philtre, in what wine, in what herb,
  Shall we drown this ancient enemy,
Destructive and gluttonous as a courtesan,
  Patient as an ant?
In what philtre?—In what wine?—In what herb?

. . . .

Can one illuminate a black and murky sky?
  Can one tear apart a darkness
Denser than pitch, without morning or evening,
  Without stars, without funereal lightning?
Can one illuminate a black and murky sky?

In such clashing and brutal lines, condensed to an overwhelming poetic compactness, we grasp in its purest form the freshness of expression peculiar to *Les Fleurs du Mal.* Here all the traditional qualities of poetry become secondary. Even euphony is no longer indispensable. This is the reason for the confusion of certain conscientious specialists who have measured this organically different composition by customary norms and have obtained disconcerting results. Baudelaire's freshness of expression is related to the newness of his inspiration. This is absolutely direct poetry. It is a poetry which offers itself as the very goal of all poetry, without ulterior motives or intermediary subjects. As inspiration springs from the heart of the poet, so poetic expression wells up from the depth of the language.

11 · *Paradis Artificiels*

"*Paradis artificiels* contains the 'philosophy' of *Les Fleurs du Mal*," wrote a contemporary of Baudelaire. This statement is perhaps exaggerated, but it is interesting. It clarifies the true nature of *Paradis artificiels*. This work does not fall into the category of a whimsical production. It is directly connected with the basic currents of Baudelaire's thought.

The subject was not in itself original. We must differentiate between those who viewed drugs as an avenue of escape from the torments of life, and those who were in search of the new sensations and the new sources of inspiration that stimulants could provide. As early as the eighteenth century, Mademoiselle de Lespinasse acquired the habit of resorting to opium "as a consolation and recourse in time of despair." For Alphonse Rabbe, Lefèvre-Deumier, Théophile Dondey, and many others, opium was primarily "an elixir of oblivion." Aside from this negative benefit, some had discovered the possibility of positive gain: "The wretched want to forget both themselves and their fate for a moment, while those who are happy seek greater happiness." Sénancour, who made this statement, seems to have been the first to consider drugs from this angle, and to make a survey of the various products which could be used for these purposes: wines and spirits, tea, coffee, tobacco, opium, betel nut, and coca. Subsequently, Thomas de Quincey in England, Hoffmann in Germany, Joubert, H. de Latouche, Eugène Sue, Barbey d'Aurevilly, and Théophile Gautier in France, had celebrated in various ways either the beneficial results of alcohol or "the delights of opium" (Eugène Sue): "an intellectual potion and celestial poison" (Latouche). Foreshadowing Baudelaire, Barbey had written in his *Memorandum* as early as 1836: "If I were a poet I would write an ode to alcohol, that Promethean fire which fills our wretched and flaccid clay with life." Joubert had even attributed spiritual effects to drunkenness: "The inebriate senses the existence of God."

The most important work dealing with the subject was written by Thomas de Quincey. *Confessions of an English Opium Eater*, a masterpiece of English prose, was introduced in France in Musset's adaptation, which he published in 1828 under his initials only, at the age of eighteen. It is known that de Quincey was impelled to use, and later to abuse, opium on account of a painful stomach ailment suffered during a period of his youth. At first opium was prescribed for him as a sedative. It later on became a necessity, as is often the case. Ultimately, opium became a source of both pleasure and suffering for him. Baudelaire was acquainted with Musset's very free translation of de Quincey's work. He himself also referred to the original, as well as to *Suspira de profundis* (Sighs from the Depths), which de Quincey had written twenty-three years after the *Confessions* as a supplement.

Baudelaire's personal experiments with opium, with hashish, and with wine were three very different kinds of experiences. A few brief details of these experiences are furnished here in order to dispel the fictions which have come to be associated with the subject. Let us begin with wine, of which he was a connoisseur—his preference for Burgundy was well known—but he used it with moderation if we trust his closest friends. "He was inclined to sobriety by nature," wrote Le Vavasseur. "We drank together often, but neither he nor I ever became tipsy." This statement deals with the period of his early youth. As to his use of wine during the remainder of his life, we can call upon the testimony of Nadar, who was his intimate friend from 1843 until his death: "During all the time that I have known him, I have never seen him drink half a bottle of unmixed wine." In the last months preceding the final crisis of 1866, he took to drinking brandy in order to abate his sufferings, and it was only then that people saw him drunk, or rather completely dazed by alcohol.

We have every reason to believe that when he wrote his poems about wine and his first essay in 1851 entitled, "Du Vin et du Hachich (*sic*) comparés comme moyens de multiplication de l'individualité" (A Comparison of Wine and Hashish as a Means of Extending Individuality), he based the piece on his study of the effects of drunkenness in others. This is the impression we get from his writings, both poetry and prose. This impression is specifically proven by the observations made in his essay, in which wine and hashish are viewed as opposing, rather than related, agents. Wine was given a much more favorable treatment. He praised its blessings in his poems as well as in his prose. He did not minimize its dangers: "What overpowering spectacles we see as a result of wine, spectacles illumined by their own interior light! How fiery and real is the second childhood that man drains from it! But at the same time, how terrifying its voluptuous delights and enervating charms." It was because of his compassion "for the working classes, who earn the right to drink it," that he saw so much good in wine: "Wine makes people benign and sociable." Similar considerations induced him to place a strict censure on the use of hashish: "It produces neither soldiers nor citizens." Hashish is "antisocial" and "tends to isolate"; "it is intended for the use of hapless idlers."

Baudelaire abandoned his essay of 1851, merely using the documented portions in his "Poëme du Haschisch" (Hashish Poem) in 1858. He had gained only part of this information from his own experiences. In the work of 1858, he himself quotes some of his sources; as far as the effects of hashish were concerned, he did not gain all his knowledge firsthand. He made ample use of medical data, referring especially to the treatise of Brierre de Boismont, *Des Hallucinations* (About Hallucinations), and the book of Moreau (de Tours) entitled *Du Haschisch et de l'aliénation mentale* (Concerning Hashish and Mental Alienation), both of which had appeared in 1845. It is true that he experimented with hashish himself. During his residence at the Hotel Pimodan between 1843 and 1846, several artists and writers who used to meet in the home of the painter Boissard tried the effects of hashish and formed a "Club des Haschischins." But this "club," the secrets of which were divulged by Gautier in the *Revue des Deux Mondes*, was not a clandestine smoking den. None of the participants, who included Baudelaire in their number, ever became intoxicated.

As for opium, the circumstances were different and could more readily be compared to those of de Quincey's case. It appears from Baudelaire's correspondence that laudanum had been prescribed for him by his doctors as a sedative and that in his "Poëme du Haschisch" we have his personal confession: "The loss of our sense of the infinite is responsible, in my opinion, for all our wicked excesses: from the heavy indulgence of the lonely man of letters, who is driven to opium as a relief from his physical sufferings, discovers in it a source of morbid pleasures, and gradually comes to look upon it as the sole ingredient of his diet and as the apex of his spiritual life; to the most loathsome drunkard, wallowing in the garbage of the gutter, his brain engulfed in flames and glory." Though Baudelaire's misuse of laudanum incurred harmful results, he does not seem to have become addicted to it. His situation was, therefore, not identical with de Quincey's, though it certainly helped him to arrive at a better understanding of the English writer.

The sentence we have just quoted reveals a completely different attitude from that of his essay of 1851, which justified "the drunkenness prevalent in the suburbs," though it did not exalt it. Baudelaire's judgment in 1851 had been dictated by social considerations. His essay of 1858 represents a landmark by which we can measure the development of his ideas during that interval.

In 1851, Baudelaire implied that drunkenness might involve a process which was opposed to the human order: "A physician who was also a true philosopher . . . could explain how and why certain beverages have the capacity of intensifying the personality of a rational being beyond measure, and of creating a third person. This is a mystic process whereby natural man and wine, respectively the animal and the vegetable deities, play the role of God the Father and God the Son in the Trinity. They generate a Holy Spirit, the superman who proceeds equally from the Father and the Son." Somewhat later in the text, he also discussed at length the weakness resulting from the use of hashish: "This is the punishment incurred through the *impious* prodigality with which you have freely consumed your nervous fluid." But the word impious, which we have italicized above, would certainly be considered a mere stylistic device by the uninitiated reader.

It is possible that Baudelaire may have had some uneasy afterthoughts as early as 1851, when he wrote the above, but they were suppressed at that time. It was in the course of the following years that his spirituality took on a definitely religious character, and his study of 1858 is one of the most explicit in this regard. The dedication and the subtitles bear this out with even greater force. This dedication, addressed to "J. G. F.," remains mysterious. What is important is that Baudelaire invoked a woman's name in grateful affection, "one who now directs all her thoughts toward Heaven, the region where all transfigurations become possible." This opening is admirably in keeping with the ensuing work.

The first part, entitled "Le goût de l'infini" (The Taste of Infinity) in 1860, was originally intended as the introduction, and therefore must be considered as dominating the entire work. It provides an explanation of the urge which prompts man to seek a state of being which elevates him above his own condition. This explanation is deliberately conducted on a metaphysical level, so that it transcends the realm of stimulants and drugs to include all the efforts directed towards freeing man from what the author calls his inherent condition. This could well be called the "philosophy" of *Les Fleurs du Mal.*

Baudelaire starts with the premise that life grants us privileged moments of "paradisial" happiness, which we do not merit. "This is why," he states in conclusion, "I prefer to consider the abnormal condition of our minds as a genuine state of grace, or as a magic mirror in which we have been invited to contemplate our enhanced image: ourselves, as we could and should be—a kind of angelic excitation. This is a call to order in a complimentary guise." It is a gratuitous gift in the religious, and even the Jansenist, sense of the word. It is to be expected that the man who has experienced these blessings, "this sharpening of the thoughts, this exaltation of the senses and of the mind," should consider them "as the most desirable good. Mindful only of his immediate pleasure, and not fearing to upset the laws of his constitution, he seeks in the physical sciences, in drugs, in the crudest alcoholic beverages and in the most delicate fragrances, in any possible climate and during any given time, the means of escaping, if only for a few hours, his miry dwelling-place. . . ." It is man's aspiration towards the infinite that causes him to stray, and his very vices, "every bit as horrifying as we imagine them to be," furnish the proof. We can recognize here the theme of "Femmes damnées," those "pursuers of the infinite . . ."

It is at this point that the Spirit of Evil makes its appearance. He is the same spirit that had harassed the good Flaubert. He is the spirit that Baudelaire made personally responsible for this vice. We have come a long way from the first draft of "Vin des chiffoniers":

> Oh the great mercy of Him whom all things praise
> Who had first given us the sweetness of slumber
> And then added Wine, child of the Sun,
> To warm our hearts again, and soothe the pain
> Of all those sorrows which die in silence. . . .

Until 1852 he had attributed wine to a gift of God. By 1857 he made radical changes:

> God, seized with remorse, created sleep;
> Man added Wine, the sacred child of the Sun.

This transformation did not imply an indictment of God. On the contrary, it relieved Him of all responsibility by placing it on the shoulders of mankind. At this point, Baudelaire considered drunkenness to be the result of Satanic temptation, no matter what momentary advantages it might provide. This change of perspective occurred during the period that Baudelaire was preparing the first edition of *Les Fleurs du Mal.* Although the text had already been transformed, the place given to the chapter on "Wine" was still favorable to drunkenness. The significance of the displacement of this chapter in the second edition is that it marks a moral and religious stand which could not be mistaken. The "Poëme du Haschisch" no longer allows man to escape sanctions and to shield himself from his destiny: "everything leads to reward and punishment, which are two forms of eternity."

The novelty of this essay is to be found in this moral judgment, founded upon a religious metaphysics. This incurred

Villemain's disapproval, according to one of Baudelaire's letters: "Toxicology, Sir, cannot be equated with Morality!" As a reply to "this colossal stupidity expressed with an air of undue solemnity," Baudelaire stated: "Doubtlessly an obvious truth, but is it not indispensable to raise the question of Morality in connection with Drugs?" In his first essay, this morality had only social implications. In 1858 it occupied a preponderant position and prompted the author to formulate his theory of the human condition. The second and third parts borrowed the substance and part of the text from the first essay. In the third part, entitled "Le Théâtre de Séraphin" (Theatre of Seraphim), an allusion to Pascal revealed the nature of Baudelaire's condemnation: "He wanted to reach angelic heights, but he became a beast instead," he said of the man who sought the intoxication of hashish. In the last two parts, "L'Homme-Dieu" (The Man-God) and "Morale" (Morality), he tackled the problem directly, in terms which leave no doubt about the importance he placed on it. "It is time that we dispense with all the hocus-pocus and elaborate make-believe contrived by the inanity of childish mentalities. Should we not discuss more serious subjects: the transformation of feelings, or, in a word, the morality of hashish?"

He begins by analyzing once more the effects of hashish. But this time, instead of examining its intellectual manifestations, he examines its spiritual consequences. Here is the second spiritual portrait that we have of the author, rendered with more soberness than that of *La Fanfarlo*. It is all the more invaluable because of the anonymity which permitted the author to shed his reticence and his usual deviousness:

"A temperament which is partly nervous and partly high-strung is most given to the development of a drunkenness of this kind. A cultivated mind, versed in the knowledge of color and form; a sensitive nature wearied by unhappiness, but still open to new influences. We concede his former mistakes and their expected consequences, consequences which result, in an easily excitable nature, in actual remorse or, if not that, at least in regret for time misused or badly employed. A penchant for metaphysics and an acquaintance with the various hypotheses of philosophy concerning human destiny are not useless. Nor is that love of virtue, stoic or mystic, which was held up by all the books of our childhood as the highest possible summit which can be reached by a distinguished man."

With the addition of "a great refinement of the senses," Baudelaire's self-portrait of 1858 is complete. It doubtless represents him much as he really was.

The action of hashish on this temperament consisted in dispelling all feelings of guilt and pardoning all errors committed in the name of virtue, or stemming from the aspiration towards virtue. In describing a person under the influence of hashish, who thereby acquires "a practical capacity for virtue through his meditations and plans to that end," Baudelaire adds, "he confused his dreams with his deeds." He was speaking here in terms of *personal* dreams and actions. But the error is very much the same as that which he described in "Le Reniement de saint Pierre":

> —Certainly, I will be quite satisfied to leave
> A world where the act is not the sister of the dream.

Baudelaire did not ascribe this spiritual meandering exclusively to the drunkenness provoked by the use of hashish. "Jean-Jacques Rousseau became drunk without hashish." In short, he was denouncing the sin of disembodiment. Hashish favored its development and brought on the paroxysm: "I have become God!" But it arises from a state of mind common to all men. This essay reinforces the interpetation that we have given to the chapter on "Révolte" in *Les Fleurs du Mal*. It is a description of feelings that the author diagnoses in himself as he would an illness. He, who so severely condemned the confusion of dreams and actions, could not approve of anything which tended to increase this confusion. Though we do find evidence of disembodiment in Baudelaire's case, we also find an awareness and condemnation of this sin as such.

This is demonstrated by the fifth and last part, in which he cites *Melmoth the Wanderer* by Charles Maturin: "Let us recall Melmoth, that magnificent symbol. His dreadful sufferings existed in the disproportion between the marvelous faculties which he acquired after a pact with the Devil, and the environment in which he was condemned to live as a creature of God. None of those whom he intends to seduce would consent to purchase that dreadful privilege under the same conditions. Indeed, all men who refuse to accept the conditions of this life sell their souls. It is easy to see the connection between the Satanic creations of poets and the living beings who have given themselves over to drugs. Behold the man who wanted to become God, sunken in no time to a level below his own, by reason of inalterable moral laws. He is a soul who sells himself by degrees."

This passage indicates that if Baudelaire was tempted to cast aside "the conditions of life," he did not succumb to this temptation. He did not believe himself innocent, and he was not "aping the sacrament of penance in a sacrilegious way, and playing the part of the sinner and the confessor simultaneously." Nor would he grant himself "a lenient absolution, or find new nourishment for his pride in his condemnation." The true character of *Les Fleurs du Mal* is elucidated by this "Poëme du Haschisch." It expressed the entire dilemma of the human condition. Baudelaire was a rebel, but a rebel only against himself. He accepted the "conditions of life," no matter how painful, because he knew what price his refusal would have cost him: "What is the good of a paradise bought at the price of eternal salvation?"

We have dispensed with the documentary and anecdotal portions of this essay, not because they are lacking in interest, but because they do not shed more light on the moral question. There is no need either to say much about the second and last part of *Paradis artificiels* entitled "Un mangeur d'opium" (An Opium Eater). "Un mangeur d'opium" is the magnificent presentation of a magnificent work. Baudelaire's comments provide an admirable framework for the extracts of the *Confessions of an English Opium Eater*, which he translated with devotion. But whatever the merits of this work—and they are considerable—they impart no new information on Baudelaire.

Les Paradis artificiels, which represents his only completed and published work besides *Les Fleurs du Mal*, is a work of the first magnitude because Baudelaire could never tackle any subject without penetrating it so completely that he discovered therein the eternal problems which have plagued both the artist and mankind.

12 · Bric-À-Brac Esthétique

THIS SAME profundity and universality also lends a permanent interest to the literary and artistic criticism which fills two volumes of the posthumous edition of Baudelaire's work: *L'Art romantique* (Romantic Art), and *Curiosités esthétiques.* Baudelaire had thought of collecting those writings as early as 1853. This intention was renewed and strengthened as the abundance of his production increased. He considered one title after another. The term *Bric-à-Brac,* with which he toyed for some time, was not a bad choice. It provided for the grouping of all his critical works under the same heading. None of the titles was wholly satisfactory. They do not express at once the great variety, and the equally remarkable unity, of these collected essays. The diversity of these pieces may be judged by a glance at the table of contents of the two volumes, adding to them the *Oeuvres posthumes* (Posthumous Works), which also contains several articles and drafts that Banville and Asselineau did not include in the edition brought out by Michel Lévy. As for their underlying unity, Baudelaire himself asserted it in a letter of 1865: "This is not a bundle of newspaper articles, as you may be inclined to think. Although these articles have appeared at lengthy intervals, they are tied together by one systematic scheme." His critical work was truly creative, following the program he had outlined in his *Salon de 1846.* All the fundamental problems of aesthetics were examined in the light of a perfectly constructed and coherent system. We can clearly distinguish the elements of a complete system of aesthetics.

Even the most far-fetched subjects, which belong to the most remote regions of the artistic domain—among them toys and laughter—were treated. One of the most surprising of the articles was entitled "Morale du Joujou" (Ethics of Toys), published in 1853, since Baudelaire rarely missed an opportunity to express his distrust of young people, and especially of children, those "budding Devils." This may have only been a defense against middle-class sentimentality on the subject. He showed nothing but generous benevolence towards the very young writers who asked his aid, such as Léon Cladel, Villiers de l'Isle Adam, and Catulle Mendès.

He took a lively interest in toys. He planned another article wherein he was to discuss "their manufacture and the tastes of various nations in this regard." A portion of his first article provided the substance for one of his prose poems, "Le Joujou du pauvre" (The Poor Man's Playthings). He also devoted two other prose poems to children: "Le Gâteau" (The Cake) and "Les Vocations" (The Vocations). He found an aesthetic element in toys, rarely in the objects themselves, but in what they represented: "The nimble ease with which children satisfy their imaginations is a proof of their spirituality in the realm of artistic conceptions. Children's first introduction to art comes through toys." The importance of this introduction to art is made evident in Baudelaire's oft-repeated statement that "Genius is childhood regained." Some statements in the article lead us to believe that he first sensed his calling as an artist through contact with toys, but his usual discretion leaves us no basis for making any definite conclusions on this subject.

The connection between laughter and art can be more readily seen, but we are surprised to find that Baudelaire's article on this subject does not deal with comedy. This essay, published in 1855, bore the title of "De l'Essence du Rire et généralement du Comique dans les arts plastiques." Baudelaire's starting point was the art of caricature, about which he had been planning to write a history, or an extensive treatise, for some time. He finally restricted himself to the completion of his study concerning "L'Essence du Rire," and to two rather short articles entitled "Quelques caricaturistes français" (Several French Caricaturists) and "Quelques caricaturistes étrangers" (Several Foreign Caricaturists), both written in 1857.

The title "De l'Essence du Rire," described the author's intentions quite well. The research he undertook was much less oriented towards psychology than towards metaphysics. Even the strictly aesthetic problem involved was ignored, though he brought it up in the beginning of the essay: "A most curious and arresting consideration is the presence of this elusive element of beauty in the very works of art which were created for the purpose of portraying man's physical and moral ugliness!" At the same time, he was attracted by another question, which also involved aesthetics, though indirectly: "And the fact that this sorry spectacle provokes in him an undying and incorrigible hilarity is not lacking in mystery either." He concerned himself with the latter question because it was linked with his most abiding and urgent preoccupation: the human condition.

It is significant that the first writers he mentioned in his study were Joseph de Maistre, Bossuet, and Bourdaloue. He treated his subject "from the point of view of the orthodox mentality," and made no secret of the fact. He pointed out that "the Sage of sages, the Incarnate Word, never laughed,"—an observation made in a poem by his friend Le Vavasseur:

> Joyous Gods, I despise you. Jesus never laughed!

He asserted with certainty "that human laughter is closely connected with the calamity brought about by an ancient fall, by a degradation which was both physical and moral. Laughter and pain are expressed by the organs in which dwell the knowledge of good and evil: the eyes and the mouth." This seems to be the first time that laughter was associated with pain as an effect occasioned by the curse of original sin. In Baudelaire's opinion, laughter was as unknown before the fall as sorrow, and these signs of our transgression also help atone for it. "And notice that it is with tears that man washes away the sufferings of man, and it is with his laughter that he pacifies and conquers his heart, for the consequences of the fall will become the means to redemption."

Hence, the comic is "an accursed element originating in Satan," "one of the clearest traces of Satan existing in man." It is a manifestation of pride. "Laughter arises from the idea of individual superiority. A Satanic notion if ever there was one!" Consequently, this comic element increases with the development of this sense of superiority. It is not a question of material progress, but of evolution towards an "absolute purification promised by certain mystic prophets." Through this purification, humanity "gains strength in return for evil and the knowledge of evil, in proportion to the strength it had gained from good."

Baudelaire chose the same example which Bergson was to use: "What is so delightful about the sight of a man who slips on ice or on the pavement, of someone who trips on a curb, that could cause such a drastic contraction on the countenance of his brother in Jesus Christ, making his facial muscles contort spasmodically like a cuckoo clock at high noon, or like a restless jack-in-the-box?" However, he was not satisfied with a naturalistic explanation as was the modern philosopher. Laughter is indeed caused by human sentiments, but these sentiments have a Satanic origin. Here again, Baudelaire found manifestations of the eternal duality of human nature: "In fact, since laughter is essentially human, it is essentially contradictory, that is to say, it denotes both infinite greatness and infinite baseness, the latter in comparison with the absolute Being whose existence he perceives, the former in comparison with animals. Laughter proceeds from the perpetual collision of these two extremes."

A like explanation will be accepted only by believers. But it would be impossible to deny that Baudelaire clarified one of the most difficult aspects of the problem. He made no attempt to gloss over its complexities. He admitted that "there are various species of laughter," and carefully distinguished laughter from joy. He indicated the special nature of children's laughter, which he likened "to the unfolding of a blossom." Finally, he recognized the somewhat less Satanic nature of laughter provoked by the absurd, which is creative, while the comic element is merely imitative. In the case of the former, laughter is still provoked by the notion of superiority, but it is the superiority of man over nature instead of the superiority of man over man. He equated the absurd with the comic element in its absolute form, while the ordinary comic element is meaningful. But he took care to specify that "if we consider the matter from the viewpoint of an absolute, there is nothing left but joy. The comic element is absolute only in relation to a fallen humanity."

The numerous examples which he furnished were preparation for a more voluminous study. In France he points to a comedy of general significance, as in Rabelais, though he did also call attention to the absurd, or absolute comic element, in some of Molière's interludes, "unfortunately too rarely read and too infrequently performed." He says that he often found this absolute comic element in the works of German, English, and Spanish writers and artists.

The two articles dealing with foreign and French caricaturists are too specific to have much general application. Their principal importance lies in the high value Baudelaire placed on Daumier at a time when public opinion was far from sharing his sentiments.

This brings us back to Baudelaire's art criticism. He did significant work in this field until 1863. That year marked the publication of "L'Oeuvre et la vie d'Eugène Delacroix," a comprehensive study written on the occasion of the artist's death, which contained definitive views about the artist and the man. It was also the year which saw the appearance of "Le Peintre de la vie moderne" (The Painter of Modern Life), an important essay completed three years before. His previous publications in the field included "l'Exposition universelle" in 1855, the *Salon de 1859*, and some shorter articles: "Peintures murales d'Eugène Delacroix à Saint-Sulpice" (Eugène Delacroix's Murals in Saint-Sulpice) which appeared in 1861 and "Peintres et aquafortistes" (Painters and Etchers), dating from 1862.

These works add the final complement to our knowledge of Baudelaire's aesthetic principles without introducing substantial alterations. Only two points previously established require slight modifications or corrections. He had now grown past his first impressions regarding David and his school, and had lost the "enormous respect which, during our childhood, had encompassed all his figures and spectres, full of fantastic power in spite of themselves." His evaluation of Ingres was also less enthusiastic in 1855 than it had been ten years earlier.

The opinion which he expressed about sculpture in his *Salon de 1859* represented an almost radical departure from the flippantly scornful attitude which he had manifested in 1846 when he wrote "Pourquoi la sculpture est ennuyeuse" (Why Sculpture is Boring). At that time he had seen in it an art closely related to nature and far removed from painting, "which is an art which requires profound contemplation, even the enjoyment of which requires a special initiation." He attributed serious disadvantages to the ill-favored art of sculpture: "It is as brutal and positive as nature, but at the same time vague and evasive. We are given too many sides to consider simultaneously." Even "after its emergence from its primitive state, sculpture, in its most magnificent achievements, is nothing but a secondary art." It can boast of no other function than "to serve as a humble partner to painting and architecture, by furthering their aims." On the other hand, in 1859 he spoke of "the divine role played by sculpture." "In the same way that lyric poetry lends an air of nobility to everything, even passion, so sculpture, genuine sculpture, invests all things, even movement, with an aura of solemnity. It endows all human creations with an eternal quality which partakes of the hardness of its substance."

He may just have changed his mind, as was within his own rights, but we are inclined to think that his new attitude might be due to the influence of Schelling. Perhaps he had not read his *Système de l'idéalisme transcendental,* as it was called in the French translation as soon as it was published in 1842. With his well-known interest in intellectual endeavors, he could have hardly ignored his dialogue, *Bruno, ou du principe divin et naturel des choses,* or his *Écrits philosophiques et morceaux propres à donner une idée générale de son système,* which were translated in 1845 and 1847, respectively. The spiritual idealism of Schelling, and the philosophy of unity which he had borrowed from Giordano Bruno (which, incidentally, bears a close relationship to Swedenborg's system of universal analogies), must have attracted Baudelaire's attention. It would otherwise be difficult to account for his famous statement concerning Delacroix in the *Salon de 1859*: "It is the infinite in the finite." This sentence can be found frequently in the writings of Schelling, who had used it in his definition of beauty in the *Écrits philosophiques*: "Beauty is the manifestation of the divine in the terrestrial, of the infinite in the finite." Now, in Schelling's opinion, sculpture could be classified as a plastic art because of its absolute nondifferentiation, that is to say, because it identifies the infinite with the finite. He referred to Winckelmann, who had placed it at the summit of the plastic arts. This hypothetical acquaintance with the works of Schelling would, if it were correct, suffice to explain Baudelaire's change of heart concerning the art of sculpture.

He held to his earlier convictions in other respects, especially with regard to his romanticism and to his belief that imagination, the "queen of all our faculties," is the key attribute of genius. "Imagination creates analysis and synthesis. . . . It has given man a practical sense of color, form, sounds, and scents. In the beginning of the world it produced analogies and metaphors. . . . Since imagination created the world (I believe one can say this, even in a religious sense), it is only just that it should have control of it." Baudelaire was not speaking of imagination in its banal sense. He even suggested a distinction he had found in an English book between two kinds of imagination, which the English language expresses with two different words: fancy and constructive imagination. The author, Catherine Crowe, was undoubtedly indebted to Hegel for this distinction (*Einbildungskraft* and *Phantasie*). Baudelaire singled out this constructive imagination as the supreme quality of the artist; it does not estrange him from reality, because it is the "epitome of truth." It dominates all other qualities, but it cannot fulfill all the requirements of art by itself. Baudelaire again defined the role of craftsmanship: "The person endowed with nothing but skill is a fool, and the imagination that tries to dispense with skill is nothing but insane."

He also gave the finishing touches to his doctrine concerning the relationship of art to nature. We have already examined the metaphysical aspect of the question, but there are also aesthetic considerations. According to the saying of Eugene

Delacroix, which Baudelaire repeated on several occasions, "nature is merely a dictionary." Only "those who have no imagination copy the dictionary." Genuine artists use it to select "the elements which are in keeping with their own conception of reality." A landscape, no matter how appealing, is never beautiful in itself, "but through my person and my own good will, the ideas or feelings I associate with it." Great artist that he was, Baudelaire could not concede that nature could become the subject of a painting, but only of a study. He had great admiration for the "liquid and airy magic" of Boudin, the painter from Honfleur; but he reminded him by way of warning that, "according to the opinion of Robespierre, a dedicated student of the humanities, 'man never ceases to look upon man with pleasure.' "

He had much to say about photography, which was heralded as a rival to the art of painting during the first outburst of enthusiasm which greeted its discovery. His protests have lost much of their interest today, but they are still remarkable. He defines the practical uses of photography and determines at the same time "its actual purpose, which is to behave as a servant to the arts and sciences, but as a very humble one, comparable to the place held by the processes of printing and stenography, which have neither created nor supplanted literature."

This leads us to another concept, that of progress, which Baudelaire had broached in his "Exposition universelle" of 1855, and to which he returned on several occasions: in his writings on Edgar Allan Poe, in his letters, and in the *Journaux intimes*. Belief in progress, that "doctrine fit for idlers," is "a very fashionable error, and one from which I want to protect myself as from hell." Hatred of progress was an almost unanimous cry sounded by the members of the School of Art for Art's Sake. But Baudelaire had already set himself apart from them, as we have seen. For him there was no progress except moral, and consequently individual, advancement. It was the indefinite idea of a kind of universal progress that he persecuted relentlessly, along with other modern "heresies." This modern concept of progress did not take into account one of the essential prerogatives of man: the liberty of choosing good or evil and their consequences. "Liberty vanishes and punishment disappears." As he stated in *Mon Coeur mis à nu*: "When every individual sets his heart on spiritual advancement, then, and only then, will humanity be on the road to progress." When that happens, liberty and fatality will be identical. In connection with this idea, one can recall another famous passage of *Mon Coeur mis à nu*:

> A Theory of True Civilization.
>
> It is not a matter of gas, or steam, or table-turning; it consists in lessening the traces left by original sin.

It was impossible for Baudelaire to treat even the most specific subject without incorporating it into his whole system of philosophy. This tendency is particularly clear in a study he devoted to an independent artist, Constantin Guys: "Le Peintre de la vie moderne." The rather noncommittal title was probably dictated by the extraordinary modesty of this painter. Guys, who never signed his works, was "a storm of modesty." "He instigated a quarrel when he found that I wanted to write about him." Baudelaire could only obtain his authorization on the express condition "that he conceal his name, and refer to his works as those of an anonymous painter." All Guys would consent to was the use of his initials. It was perhaps for this reason that Baudelaire's piece took on such an arresting character and vast scope that it transcended the limits of an individual study. It became the pinnacle of his aesthetic edifice, and contained some of his most original discoveries.

One of the most important of these was embodied in the title, which introduced his notion of "modern" art. This concept had to do with a certain quality in the work which Baudelaire described by the newly-coined word, "modernity." The term was ambiguous and liable to misinterpretation. It is evident that no epoch is more modern than another. But Baudelaire was attempting to solve one of the most perplexing problems of aesthetics, that of relative and absolute beauty. He succeeded through a compromise which enabled him to determine their respective domains:

"Beauty is made up of an element which is eternal and unchanging, the extent of which is extremely difficult to establish, and of an element which is relative and circumstantial, and which could include at will one or all of the following: the epoch, its fashions, morals, and tastes. Without this second element, which is like the exciting, enticing, and appetizing frosting of a cake, the basic ingredient would be indigestible, unpalatable, and unsuited to human nature."

Constantin Guys was a draftsman rather than a genuine painter. But Baudelaire found in him the ideal artist that he had been hoping to encounter since 1846: one who would be able to express "the heroic nature of modern life." This again demonstrates the consistency of his thinking. Apparent contradictions in his articles disappear when we examine them more closely. We need simply to relate them to his whole philosophy in order to discover their true meaning. "Le Peintre de la vie moderne" is a good example of this.

In this piece, as in all his critical works, he did not tie himself down to a methodical exploration of his subject. For him, criticism remained a creative operation. The only difference between criticism and poetry is that criticism is brought to bear on a work of art instead of being applied directly to phenomena: "The moral considerations arising from the sketches of the artist constitute, in many cases, the best possible employment of the art of criticism." Once more he remained in accord with his earlier statements.

His freedom in dealing with the subject allows him to elucidate his most basic metaphysical convictions. We are reminded of Samuel Cramer's exclamation in *La Fanfarlo*: "Hey, don't forget your make-up!" and all the anecdotes about Baudelaire's penchant for artificial contrivances and his horror of nature. He reviewed these matters in "Le Peintre de la vie moderne" and placed them in their true perspective. Nothing could be more significant than the opening lines of his "Éloge du maquillage" (Tribute to Make-up):

"Most of the errors connected with beauty were caused by the false conception of morality which existed in the eighteenth century. Nature was then considered to be the basis, the source and the model of the ideal and of the most beautiful. The general short-sightedness of that century was due in no small part to its denial of original sin."

We have now penetrated to the center of Baudelaire's thought. All of his works were governed by his awareness of sin.

"All literature is a by-product of sin." This is the reason why nature, which "shared in original sin," must be controlled and spiritualized by art. "Nature teaches nothing, or almost nothing. . . . All that is noble and beautiful is the result of reason. Crime . . . was natural from the very beginning, while virtue, on the other hand, is *artificial* and supernatural. . . ." Baudelaire was, therefore, invoking virtue and morality, that is to say, artificiality, when he sang the praises of "the supreme spirituality of the *toilette*" and the propriety of make-up. "Women are well within their rights when they strive for magic and supernatural effects; they are even fulfilling a kind of obligation by so doing." The word "supernatural" precisely indicates the nature of the desired transformation: eyebrow pencil "gives the eye the appearance of a window opening on the infinite," while rouge "endows the feminine countenance with the mysterious passion of a high-priestess."

It is not our duty to determine whether these corollaries of Baudelaire's spirituality are valid or not. We merely wish to comprehend the rigorous logic that has formulated them. Let us further examine Baudelaire's views on women. We may recall the observation in *Mon Coeur mis à nu*: "Woman is *natural*, and therefore abominable. At the same time she is common, that is to say, the opposite of a dandy." She is abominable *because* she is natural. However, she can soften this imperfection by means of her make-up and *toilette*. "In a word, for artists in general, and M. G. in particular, woman does not merely signify the feminine counterpart of man. Rather, she is a divinty and a heavenly star which presides over all the activities of the male mind; she is the reflection of all nature's charms contained in one being; she is the object of the greatest admiration and of the most animated curiosity that the spectacle of life can offer to the spectator." This exaltation of women does not nullify his previous statements. The metaphysical arguments which he used to condemn women and nature are identical, but metaphysics and feeling are two different things and what is said of one should not be applied to the other.

Though women were able to rehabilitate themselves to some extent through artifice or by an "alteration of nature," they were incapable of ascending to the heights of dandyism.

This was a serious flaw, for in the vocabulary of our author this word has a mystic significance. Dandyism had been his constant preoccupation. By it he did not mean merely a preoccupation with dress or matters of exterior consequence. The importance he attached to it can be perceived from the article which he was planning to write on the subject from 1860 until the last moments of his literary activity. Joseph de Maistre, the Marquis de Custine, Liszt, Ferrari, Paul de Molènes, and Barbey d'Aurevilly were to have been included as subjects of study, but it was Chateaubriand, "the father of all dandies," who was to have been its chief exponent. His name was incorporated into most of the tentative titles. When we consider Baudelaire's undying admiration for Chateaubriand, the importance he attached to the concept of dandyism can more readily be inferred. Unfortunately, Baudelaire never wrote this article, but he did devote a chapter to dandyism in "Le Peintre de la vie moderne." This chapter, when studied in conjunction with certain passages of his *Journaux intimes*, gives us an understanding of what he meant by this term.

We can detect a stoic tendency in Baudelaire's dandyism. This trait is implicit in the first subtitle he planned to use for the projected article: "Le Dandysme littéraire, ou la Grandeur sans convictions" (Literary Dandyism, or Grandeur without Convictions). It is also evident in his statement about Constantin Guys: "One can see that in certain aspects dandyism borders on spiritualism and stoicism." Dandyism was "a sort of religion," of a not too orthodox kind, for it seems to have been sought only for personal gratification. "The Dandy should strive to be sublime without fail; he should live and sleep before a mirror."

Is it necessary to point out that dandyism is not simply elegance? Nor does it consist merely in "an immoderate taste for fine dress and elegant surroundings. Those things are, for the true dandy, only the symbols of the aristocratic superiority of his spirit." This very elegance demands "absolute simplicity," for one of the essential traits of this dandyism is generosity. It is a discipline which excludes all hidden thoughts of profit or reward. In the domain of love the dandy is gifted above all others, but this is, quite simply, because he alone is capable of apprehending love in its ideal form.

Where does this generosity stop? It is not very easy to determine. When Baudelaire spoke of a "grandeur without convictions," he was very close to stoicism, in the limited sense of that word, a stoicism which renounces all divine intercession. But he also wrote that the dandy should live "before a mirror." The *Journaux intimes* contain two similar versions of one idea: "To be a great man and a saint *for oneself*, that is the only thing that matters." This statement is very similar to the one quoted above. Between the first and second of these we find the "Prayer," which concludes with this sentence: "Give me strength to fulfill immediately my daily obligations, and thus to become a hero and a saint." Surely the aspirations toward heroism and sainthood are not unrelated, though only one is explicitly religious. Baudelaire's reticence concerning his intimate sentiments makes it impossible for us to assume anything definite on this point. He may perhaps have written the earlier statements during moments of doubt which, as we have seen, did occur, even in this period of growing faith. A letter addressed to his mother in May, 1861, shows us such a moment: "What about God? you would exclaim. I wish to believe with all my heart (no one will ever know the full extent of my sincerity as well as I!) that an exterior and invisible being takes an interest in my welfare; but how can I believe this?"

Nevertheless, we must realize that even at such times his spirituality continued to manifest itself. This explains his association of spiritualism and dandyism. We recall the first sentence of *Fusées*: "Even if God did not exist, Religion would still be Holy and *Divine*." Baudelaire's dandyism may be defined as the expression of a religion which has remained holy and divine in the absence of God.

Contrary to expectations, Baudelaire's literary criticism is less interesting and varied than his art criticism; he was less at ease in this domain. However, we do not accuse him of sycophancy or hypocrisy, as some have done. When he casually humored a Victor Hugo or a Gautier with silence, or enveloped his reservations concerning them with subtle discretion, he was not motivated by self-interest, but by a sincere admiration and an unwillingness to offend them or to play into the hands of their adversaries. He was harder on Hugo in his letters than he was in his criticism. In a letter to his mother he even boasted that in his article on *Les Misérables* he had proven that he had mastered "the art of lying." In some ways, this book must have struck him as being "filthy and stupid," and he took good care not to divulge his full opinion of it. But his thoughtfulness may be ascribed to his enduring respect for Hugo, a respect which did exist in spite of all that separated the two writers. Concerning *Les Misérables,* he did point out "the many instances of deliberate cheating or unconscious partiality which a strictly philosophical viewpoint could discover in Hugo's manner of presenting the terms of the problem." This was after all his main objection to the novel, the qualities of which could not escape him.

We have no reason to question the sincerity of his compliments. Upon his arrival in Brussels he paid a visit to Victor Hugo, who was then living there in exile. "I thought that a French writer could not dispense with a visit to Victor Hugo," he wrote to Sainte-Beuve. A young Belgian who recorded his observations bore witness to Baudelaire's "heartfelt reverence" for Hugo: "He is dazzled by the fertile genius of this writer." At the Hotel des Colonnes, on the Waterloo battlefield, he asked scores of questions about the poet's stay there, and expressed a desire to see his room; at dinner time he ordered "Victor Hugo's customary fare . . . Just surprise us when you serve it!"

We are also aware that Baudelaire's admiration for Gautier was limited; he hardly disguised his scorn for the poet's serial productions in his lengthy Notice of 1859. He made it clear that Gautier's aesthetic principles, no matter how noble, were different from his own. He did not even hesitate to declare that "the importance given to Beauty in *Mademoiselle de Maupin* was excessive."

It is interesting to note that his admiration of Gautier, as well as of Victor Hugo, was based chiefly on those qualities which coincided with his own convictions. Though he valued their virtuosity, he attributed their real greatness as poets, in Gautier's case to his "innate perception of universal Correspondence and symbolism," and in Hugo's to his "recognition of universal analogies." Just as he was the first to hail Balzac as a visionary rather than as an observer, so in Hugo's works he praised above all his expression of "life's mystery," suggested, he added, "with the necessary obscurity." In short, it was also the visionary Hugo that he esteemed above all, and here again, as in his evaluations of contemporary painting, his statements proved to be prophetic of later criticism. He now accorded to Hugo what he had denied him in 1846: that necessary margin of imaginative genius which he took to be a sign of genius. We note that Hugo's *La Légende des Siècles* (The Legend of the Ages) had been published in the intervening period.

One more significant detail should be noted in Baudelaire's appraisals of Hugo and Gautier: Baudelaire felt himself called upon to ascribe his own preoccupations to them although they are not too explicit about them. In light of the importance he gave to these preoccupations, this is proof of his high regard for them. He pointed out that one could accuse Gautier of a "lack of religious or political consciousness." But he immediately added, "I could, if I felt so inclined, write a new article which would refute this unjust error victoriously." He also denied other charges sometimes made against Gautier. Many had accused him of coldness and lack of humanity, and of making concessions to "His Majesty Progress, and His Most Powerful Queen, Industry." Baudelaire beseeched the reader not to judge Gautier from surface appearances and to realize that here is the only sign of a superior scorn.

At the end of his article on *Les Misérables*, Baudelaire demonstrated that Victor Hugo was not so far removed from religious orthodoxy as one would have thought. "I believe that even for those who find a comprehensive, if not a complete, explanation of the perplexing mysteries of life in orthodox teaching and Catholic theories, Victor Hugo's new book should be *Bienvenu* (Welcome) (as the bishop whose triumphant charity it portrays); this is a book to be thankful for and to acclaim. Is it not useful for the poet and the philosopher to grab self-seeking Happiness by the hair from time to time, and say to him, while shaking his ugly face above the blood and filth, 'Look at your work, and drink it!' "

It is not our task to determine whether Baudelaire's interpretations are correct, or whether he had injected a bit of his own malice into his last observation. Suffice it to say he felt the need to make it. He was unable to justify a work that was devoid of spirituality and Catholicism. Not that he was searching for declarations of orthodox faith, but it was necessary that the work partake of at least some of his convictions for him to appreciate it. He seems to have found some of these convictions in the work of Laclos and Nerciat, if we can judge from the notes he had made about them for future articles. These articles were never written, but with one of them, an article on *Les Liaisons dangereuses,* he toyed from 1856 until the last years of his life. He not only held the novel up as "a moralistic work, on a par with the most elevated and the most profound examples of the genre," but he admired it for its frank description of evil as such. "Conscious evil is less hideous and can be more easily healed than unconscious evil. G. Sand inferior to de Sade." His extremely brief notes on Nerciat are in the same vein: "The libertines of the 80's condemned themselves firmly and logically. The liberals of today don't even dare declare themselves atheists; they are betting *for* and *against* God simultaneously."

One of the texts where we can follow his thinking most clearly is an article which he published on April 1st, 1861 on Richard Wagner, titled "Richard Wagner and Tannhäuser in Paris." This article "was put together in three days in a printing shop," but it is an "occasional piece which has been given much thought." In the beginning of 1860, Baudelaire had first become enchanted by fragments of *The Flying Dutchman, Tannhäuser,* and *Lohengrin,* and the article was written on March 18, 1861, five days after the first complete performance of *Tannhäuser* in Paris. As early as 1849, probably because of Champfleury's and Barbara's influence, he had admired Wagner and hailed him as one "whom posterity will single out as the most illustrious of composers." Nevertheless, his acquaintance with Wagner's work was probably very incomplete. The performances of 1860 and 1861 were instrumental in increasing his enthusiasm and prompting him to write this article on a subject that he was not at all qualified to treat. This is precisely why this study is interesting. Wagner's music had affected him deeply. He deftly analyzed its evocative power and the images it conjured up. He was especially struck by the over-all power of the operas and of *Tannhäuser* above all. In this work he discovered the fundamental themes of his own thought. "*Tannhäuser* represents the struggle of two opposing principles who have selected the human soul as their battlefield: the flesh against the spirit, hell against heaven, and Satan against God." He did not deny the fact that these were simply the sentiments which the music called up from his own being. "Every well-developed mind carries within itself two extremes, heaven and hell, and in the totality of each of these he immediately recognizes half of himself. After the Satanic titillation of a vague love soon follow enthusiasm, astonishment, cries of triumph, groans of appreciation, and then howls of ferocity, the reproaches of the victim, and the impious hosannas of the sacrificer, as if savagery must always have its place in the drama of love, and the pleasures of the flesh had always led, with ineluctable, Satanic logic, to the delights of crime." These areas of shadow were present in Wagner, but it was the light that predominated: "When the religious theme wages a battle against raging evil, re-establishes order, and asserts its power, then it triumphs again in all its unshakable beauty amidst the chaos of dying sensual delights, and the entire spirit is rejuvenated as if by the beatitude of redemption. . . ."

For a man who "did not know music, and whose entire musical experience was confined to the performance . . . of a few lovely fragments from Weber and Beethoven," Baudelaire gave evidence of a remarkable insight when he placed Wagner in the first rank of great composers. But it was not the music alone which stirred him to this extent; it was the fact that the music was the result of a mentality so similar to his own. This study enlarges the scope of Baudelaire's aesthetic system to include all the forms of art.

13 · *Prose Poems*

IT IS DIFFICULT to determine exactly when Baudelaire first contemplated writing his prose poems. The idea must have occurred to him quite early. But not until 1855 did he publish the first two. In 1857 he talked about a volume of "Poëmes nocturnes" (Poems of the Night) as one of his projects. He published six of them under this title in *Le Présent* on August 24, 1857, just after the closing date of his trial in connection with *Les Fleurs du Mal.* This title, "Poëmes nocturnes," was used until 1861, in spite of the fact that only one of the pieces, "Le Crépuscule du soir" (Evening Twilight), justified the nocturnal appellation. "La Solitude" (Solitude), "Projets" (Projects), "L'Horloge," "La Chevelure," and "L'Invitation au voyage" did not fit this title at all. Later he included nine of these poems (of which only three were new) in the *Revue Fantaisiste* of November 1st, 1861, calling them simply "Poëmes en prose" (Poems in Prose). He apparently did not consider this title satisfactory. With regard to the prose poems, he had never entertained the idea of a book with a beginning and an end. It does seem, nevertheless, that he made an attempt to group them according to a general scheme. He toyed with the following titles: *Le Promeneur solitaire* (The Solitary Walker), *Le Rôdeur parisien* (The Vagrant of Paris), *La Lueur et la Fumée* (The Light and the Mist), or, "a title which explains my idea well," *Rêvasseries* (Daydreams). His concern for unity was in conflict with the diversity of these texts, which compelled him to reject all titles with specific references. In August and

September of 1862, he published twenty prose poems in *La Presse*. They appeared under the perfectly neutral designation of "Petits Poëmes en prose" and were preceded by a dedication to Arsène Houssaye. In the dedicatory note he emphasized the peculiar structure of this work: "If you remove a vertebra, the two pieces of this tortuous caprice would unite without difficulty. Break it into many pieces, and you will see that each can exist by itself."

His letters of March, 1863 contained for the first time the generally accepted title of these poems: *Le Spleen de Paris* (The Spleen of Paris). This title was not his final choice, despite the fact that he never abandoned it, referring to it in a letter dated February 16, 1866, several days before his first serious attack. In the publication of 1863, he again used the title *Petits Poëmes en prose*. It turned up again in November, 1864, between two references to *Spleen de Paris*. Finally, he sent two prose poems to the *Revue du XIXe siècle*, just before his attack, under the title of "Petits Poëmes lycanthropes" (Small Lycanthropic Poems). This title bears witness to his fidelity to Pétrus Borel, whom he also mentions in his notes on *Pauvre Belgique* (Poor Belgium). Considering the many changes the work had undergone, and the fact that it was never finished, it would be unwise to try to look upon its traditional title as a key to Baudelaire's intentions. It would be more advisable to accept the collection of poems for what it is, an unfinished work, and to study its contents accordingly, without trying to find an over-all scheme.

Paris certainly does play a part in the work, but a very limited one. The "Epilogue," written in tercets, is dedicated to Paris. But it is an unfinished poem which may perhaps have been written for another volume. It treats, in the same metric form, the subject he had envisaged in 1860 for the epilogue of *Les Fleurs du Mal*.

These prose poems are extremely varied, and there are lists of others, unwritten ones, in Baudelaire's papers. Some of them, such as "Une Mort héroïque" (A Heroic Death) and "La Corde" (The Rope), have the makings of short stories. Others, such as "Les Veuves" (The Widows) and "Le vieux Saltimbanque" (The Old Clown), deal with street scenes. Dialogues and symbolic narratives can also be found, for example in "Assommons les pauvres!" (Down with the Poor!), "Le galant Tireur" (The Gallant Rifleman), "Le mauvais Vitrier" (The Wicked Glazier). There are fantasy stories such as "Chacun sa Chimère" (To Each His Chimera), "Les Dons des Fées" (The Fairies' Gifts), "Perte d'Auréole" (The Loss of a Halo), and "Le Joueur généreux" (The Generous Gambler), as well as meditations and reveries. Two or three of the poems were clearly inspired by Edgar Allan Poe: "Une Mort héroïque" and "Laquelle est la vraie?" (Which Is the Real One?) are among these. But almost all of them were specifically Baudelaire's creations and do not resemble any previous attempts in the same genre.

Prose poems had been attempted in the eighteenth century. In his famous *Réflexions critiques sur la Poésie et sur la Peinture* (Critical Reflections on Poetry and Painting), written in 1719, Abbé Du Bos compared engravings "to prose Novels, containing the invention and style of Poetry." He added: "There are beautiful Poems without verse, just as there are beautiful verses without poetry, or beautiful paintings without rich coloring." But we have no need to go back so far, since Baudelaire explicitly indicated his sources in his dedication to Arsène Houssaye. Just as Aloysius Bertrand had introduced his *Gaspard de la Nuit* as a series of "fantasies in the manner of Rembrandt or Callot," so Baudelaire, in a letter of February, 1861, announced his *Poëmes nocturnes* as "Essays of lyric poetry in prose, in the same vein as *Gaspard de la Nuit*." This masterpiece by the unfortunate Bertrand appeared only after his death in 1842, and then only because of the interest of Victor Pavis and Sainte-Beuve. Although Baudelaire spoke of it only in reference to his prose poems, this work had greatly influenced him. "It was while thumbing through the famous *Gaspard de la Nuit* for the twentieth time . . . that I got the idea of trying something similar. . . ." he stated in his dedication.

This dedication took the form of a letter and included a declaration of principle, as did his first dedication of *Les Fleurs du Mal*. It too took a modest attitude towards the originality of his work. He explained himself more freely in it, since the personage concerned was not among the ranks of the living; his manner was sincere beyond a doubt, and remained both humble and proud. As he stated, his "starting point" was indeed *Gaspard de la Nuit,* but Bertrand's method was applied to a completely different subject. "As soon as I had begun my work I noticed that not only was I far away from my mysterious and brilliant model, but also that I was doing something (if it could be called *something*) remarkably different, an accident that could no doubt go to the head of someone different from myself, but which could cause me nothing but deep humiliation, for I feel that the poet's most honorable task consists in the *exact* realization of a proposed project." The form he lent to his prose poems was the necessary result of his genius, independent of all preconceived notions. He had not only strayed far afield from his model, but he had surpassed it.

His first attempts in this field perhaps began with *La Fanfarlo*. "Instead of admiring the flowers, Samuel Cramer, who felt the sting of inspiration, set himself to translating into prose, and then reciting, a few shoddy verses written in his first manner." If this sentence is ambiguous, the passages it introduced developed the style of the prose poems, as the following lines indicate: "Let your imagination listen to the brisk melodies of this mysterious keyboard. The scents of the storm float in through the windows. It is the season when the gardens are dotted with pink and white garments, unperturbed by a few raindrops. The friendly bushes clasp the fleeing robes; brown hair and blond locks become entangled in a whirl!" Here one encounters the form borrowed from Aloysius Bertrand, set in a slightly different compass and aiming directly for a poetic effect.

After this one attempt, it seemed that Baudelaire had abandoned all attempts in this genre. Then suddenly, in 1855, in a most unexpected fashion, and without introductions or explanations, he published his first two prose poems: "Le Crépuscule du soir" and "La Solitude." In the letter he addressed to Fernand Desnoyers in order to "cap" his contribution, he announced "two poetic pieces," that is to say "Les deux Crépuscules" (The Two Twilights), in verse, and did not make the slightest mention of the two additional pieces. Was this shyness, or a lack of assurance about their worth? Probably neither, as they were signed. It is more likely that he decided to include them at the last moment.

These two texts in 1855 differed greatly from their final forms. They constituted one poem divided in two parts, significantly shorter, the first in particular, than the 1864 version included in the posthumous edition of his works. The most striking variation lay in the fact that they were divided into stanzas of almost equal length, similar to *Gaspard de la Nuit*. The tone, as well as the subject, was quite different; they were more intimately linked with immediate reality. However, Baudelaire had not as yet perfected the medium.

It actually did involve a new medium concerned with new material. Upon close examination, we realize that most of the subjects treated in *Le Spleen de Paris* would not readily lend themselves to the poetic form, at least as Baudelaire had used it. Only five or six subjects are present in both *Les Fleurs du Mal* and *Le Spleen de Paris*. These constitute examples of his versatility; the same subject is developed in different ways. Some critics have considered the theory that the prose poems were earlier versions of Baudelaire's poetic ideas, sketches which were later to be translated into verse. Some went so far as to say that Baudelaire was not a real poet, since he thought in prose. This argument is of no great value in itself. Vigny, among others, often made a prose sketch as a first draft of his poems. We do not know whether Baudelaire ever did this, but his prose poems are not the results of such a method. The passage of *La Fanfarlo* that we have quoted indicates a different mode of procedure, that of *translating into prose* "a few shoddy verses." In this particular case, the verses involved might possibly be an early poem, of which we possess only four lines, but which is evocative of the passage in *La Fanfarlo*:

> He liked to watch her, with her white skirts,
> Running among the foliage and branches,
> Awkward and full of grace, as she covered
> Her legs, if her dress caught on the shrubs . . .

La Fanfarlo provides another example of poetry translated into prose in the paragraph beginning "The weather was as dark as the tomb. . . ." A certain poem, signed by Prarond, which had appeared in the 1843 collection of verse by the Norman School was its source. Let us quote only the first two lines:

> The gutter, funeral bed and destination of loathing,
> Bubblingly carries off the secrets of the sewers. . . .

and the corresponding sentence in *La Fanfarlo*:

"The gutter, funeral bed and destination of love letters and last night's orgies, bubblingly carried off its thousand secrets toward the sewers. . . ."

This is one of the strongest pieces of evidence which has been brought forward by those who support the theory of Baudelaire's clandestine participation in the Norman School collection. It does not prove their case, for Baudelaire may have drawn on poems which were not his own. He may also have written a few lines for Prarond's poem. This is of little consequence. What does matter is that the prose text *followed* the verse composition. We have every indication that the prose version of "L'Invitation au voyage" was also later than the poem in *Les Fleurs du Mal*. The poem seems to have been conceived in the beginning of 1848. The later prose version, published two years after the poem, is much more extensively developed. Holland is mentioned in specific detail, which Baudelaire had probably garnered from articles, or from an exhibition that had come to his attention in the intervening period. Baudelaire left us a sketch of the poem in the epilogue written as a contribution to the *Revue de Deux Mondes*. The second part of this poem became the basis of "L'Héautontimorouménos." It has nothing in common with the prose poems. Baudelaire himself anticipated this criticism. He told Arsène Houssaye about the great difficulties of the genre, "especially if one is to avoid giving the impression that one is presenting a first draft for a poem."

These considerations are secondary to the essential point, that is, the basic difference between the prose poems and *Les Fleurs du Mal*. From Fénelon to the present time, all those who have ventured into this realm wished to prove above all that rhyme and measure were not indispensable to poetry. Prose poems retained "the invention and the style of poetry," according to the words of Abbé Du Bos. They sought the effects of poetic harmony through the arrangement of the words and through the rhythmic cadences and effects of prose. Such experiments were often eloquent. Music obtained in this way could convey rich and profound thoughts endowed with their full meaning, or it could be a mere accompaniment bereft of melody, an oral camouflage comparable to the deceptive appearance of stage settings. Not even Chateaubriand avoided this danger at all times.

Aloysius Bertrand perfected the prose poem technique. He invested it with great subtlety by trying to obtain the closest possible equivalent of the verse poem. One can evaluate his achievement by comparing his polished pieces to the poetic prose of Alphonse Rabbe or Maurice de Guérin, who stayed within the tradition of the rhythmical sentence. But, no matter how perfect his achievements were in the genre, their effects are almost always of an exterior nature. Description is used extensively; it seems to have been created with a chisel. The object of his prose poems is almost the same as that of verse, but the orchestration is different.

These prose poems seem to have been Baudelaire's starting point, both from his own statement and from the examples in *La Fanfarlo* and the texts of 1855. We can note that the prose poems which were also developed in verse became the subjects of his first attempts: "Le Crépuscule du soir," "Un Hémisphère dans une Chevelure," and "L'Invitation au voyage" were three of the six that were published in 1857. "Les Veuves," which reworked the theme of "Les Petites Vieilles" (The Little Old Women), appeared in 1861. "A une Heure du matin (At One O'Clock in the Morning) and "La belle Dorothée" correspond to "L'Examen de minuit" (Examination of Conscience at Midnight) and "Bien loin d'ici," respectively. The difference between the prose and verse poems is in the dimension of the tone and in the movement. Baudelaire quickly understood that there was nothing to be gained by competing with poetry on its own grounds. His dedication of 1862 is a clear proof of this. What he looked for and found was "the miracle of a poetic prose, musical without the aid of rhythm and rhyme, flexible and brutal enough to conform to the lyric transports of the soul, to the gentle flow of reverie, and to the sudden starts of conscience."

Yet the technique of the prose poems bears a resemblance to the technique of *Les Fleurs du Mal,* insofar as its essential novelty is concerned. This technique was revolutionary because it employed the *internal* resources of language in their full range. But in *Les Fleurs du Mal* he retained the external resources as well. These he abolished almost completely in his prose poems. In them, Baudelaire allowed himself no recourse to the effects of poetic harmony and rhythm. His definition of 1862, quoted above, excluded such effects; he wished to achieve his aims "without rhythm and rhyme." His statement should be examined with care, for it contains the secret of this new form of expression. If this prose is musical, it is not so in the usual sense of the word. The wholly interior music no longer emanates from the imagination but from the spirit. In "*the lyric transports of the soul, the gentle flow of reverie, and the sudden starts of conscience,*" lie the origins of this harmony. It is a matter of communicating these transports directly, using only the means available to prose: the content and syntactic arrangement of the words. Baudelaire cast aside not only rhythm, but the effects of sonority and euphonic harmony. In these poems sound is of no great importance. Their poetic quality lies in the jarring effect they produce on our feelings, which is achieved by a condensation of the sentence to its active elements. This anticipates Rimbaud's "diamond-like prose," but its feline suppleness and rich timbre are Baudelaire's own.

The poetic effect is thus directly related to the emotion, or, more precisely, to the inward *motion* of the author. No matter what the subject, the result is achieved only if he expresses a profoundly felt movement of the soul. In general, the tone is more direct than in *Les Fleurs du Mal.* Some of his most profoundly moving utterances can be found in this volume. When he mentions his aesthetic problems in "Le *Confiteor* de l'artiste" (The Artist's *Confiteor*), his disclosures are more intimate than they were in his "Hymne à la Beauté." "My nerves are too tense to give other than clamoring and dolorous vibrations . . . . Ah, must one eternally suffer, forever be a fugitive from beauty? Nature, pitiless enchantress, ever victorious rival, leave me! Tempt my desires and my pride no more! The contemplation of beauty is a duel where the artist screams with terror before being vanquished."

Compare the conclusion of "L'Examen de minuit":

> Quick, let us snuff out the lamp, so that
> We can hide ourselves in the shadows.

with the harrowing lines which we find at the end of "A une Heure du matin":

> Discontented with everything, and discontented with myself, I should be glad enough to redeem myself and restore my pride a little in the silence and the solitude of the night. Souls of those whom I have loved, souls of those whom I have sung, fortify me, sustain me, drive far from me the lies and the corrupting vapors of the world; and thou, Lord my God, grant me the grace to produce a few beautiful lines which will prove to me that I am not the worst of men, that I am not lower than those I despise!

The personal character of the prose poems did not exclude the introduction of exterior or fantastic subjects, as long as they corresponded to a profound disturbance of his feelings. Thus the presence of Evil, no matter where he finds it, always causes a personal reaction in Baudelaire, both of pity and of reminiscence. Though his style was as direct as possible, the subject could still be treated indirectly through the use of symbols, or through a kind of sustained metaphor. In order to make a stronger impression on the reader, Baudelaire did not hesitate to use violent means. For example, in "Le mauvais Vitrier," the need for an ideal and the rejection of a tainted reality are expressed through the oblique ways of a cruel and sadistic imagination. But sadism and other forms of Evil are only mysterious tests which, in "Mademoiselle Bistouri," evoke Baudelaire's most painful and moving prayer:

> Life swarms with innocent monsters. —Lord, my God! thou, the Creator; thou, the Master; thou who made Law and Liberty; thou, the Sovereign who does not interfere; thou, the Judge who pardons all; thou who art full of motives and causes, and who has perhaps placed in my spirit a taste for horror in order to convert my heart, like a healing balm placed on the end of a sword; Lord, have mercy, have mercy on mad men and women! O Creator! Can there be monsters in the eyes of Him who knows why they exist, how

they have come into existence, and how it would have been possible for them *not to exist*?

The examples above clearly demonstrate the direct communication that the prose poem tried to establish between the author and the reader. But the style of these examples is that of lyric tenderness, and does not adequately convey the novelty of this poetic prose. The most striking specimen of this novelty is found in the first poem of the volume. "L'Étranger" (The Stranger), which produces a poetic climate of peerless intensity in its brief and incisive responses.

This "unusual" book, as Baudelaire described it, troubled him. "Ah! What great frustration and toil accompanied the composition of *Spleen*! And I am still not satisfied with some parts!" In spite of his efforts, he was unable to bring the work to completion. He announced to his mother, in the early part of 1866, that he intended to "work on it actively for two weeks." Though he had planned a hundred poems, the posthumous edition contains only half that number. It is therefore impossible to compare this work with *Les Fleurs du Mal*, for which it was to function as a companion piece. Nevertheless, it is also impossible to separate the two books. They flow from the same aesthetic principles. We must link them together in order to fully grasp Baudelaire's supreme originality.

14 · Pauvre Belgique

THE PUBLICATION OF twenty "Petits Poëmes en prose" in *La Presse* during 1862 established Baudelaire's reputation. This does not mean that the reception of the public was particularly warm. Was it the novelty of the genre which disconcerted the readers? None of his productions had been more difficult to sell to newspapers and magazines than these were. Their publication in the *Figaro* was interrupted during 1864 "simply because my poems were boring everyone." He offered them to four or five periodicals with no success. Of the eleven that he submitted to the *Revue Nationale* in 1865, five were rejected as "unpublishable." The rest did not appear until shortly after his death.

But the experts did not misjudge them. It was Hetzel who wrote to Arsène Houssaye: "Read this carefully.—I would like to write this to you in flaming characters—you have the first of Baudelaire's prose poems, and they must be printed in a newspaper before I can publish them. Baudelaire is our old friend—which means nothing because we are plagued with friends—but he is also the most original prose writer and the most individual poet of our times—no newspaper should delay the publication of this strange classic poet who deals with unclassical subjects—get it into print quickly, therefore—quickly, and notify me to that effect."

Sainte-Beuve referred to "Le vieux Saltimbanque" and "Les Veuves" as "jewels." Baudelaire had won the respect of all men of letters. He had published in close sequence his *Paradis artificiels* and the second edition of *Les Fleurs du Mal.* In publishing the fourth volume of his anthology which dealt with contemporary figures, Eugène Crépet included seven of Baudelaire's poems, and asked Théophile Gautier to write the introduction to them. He also commissioned Baudelaire to write the most important introductions, those dealing with Victor Hugo, Gautier, Banville, Leconte de Lisle, and Marceline Desbordes-Valmore. Therefore, Baudelaire's aspiration toward the French Academy should not surprise us very much. He mentioned the Academy to his mother in July, 1861 for the first time. "Several people are urging me to submit my candidature to the Academy." He sent his official application to the Permanent Secretary on December 11 of that year. It is worthy of note that of a possible choice between the seats of Scribe and Lacordaire, he decided for the seat of Lacordaire, "because he was a religious man and a Romantic." He withdrew his candidature two months later on the advice of Sainte-Beuve and Vigny. His application must certainly have surprised quite a few of those gentlemen of the Academy to whom Baudelaire was either completely unknown or a kind of brazen amateur. He was, however, well received by several of the significant members: Lamartine, Jules Sandeau, Vigny, and even Monsieur Patin. As Sainte-Beuve stated, the Academy as a whole was "more surprised than shocked." As for outside literary figures, if they predicted his defeat, it was not because they were lacking in respect for Baudelaire. In reviewing the list of candidates, one of them accorded a special mention to "Monsieur Baudelaire, a courageous poet, translator of Edgar Poe, who is himself the Edgar Poe of the old world. If all the windows of Mazarin's venerable palace do not break into a thousand pieces on the occasion of Monsieur Baudelaire's solemn reception under that dome, we will then have to acknowledge the fact that the god of classical tradition has conclusively passed away or disappeared." In spite of his disapproval of Baudelaire's candidature, Sainte-Beuve himself referred to him quite favorably in his article of January 20th "Des prochaines élections à l'Académie" (Concerning the Next Elections to the Academy).

What was the cause of his withdrawal? Probably the certain lack of success. Another reason may have been his failing health, which began to concern him more than anything else. The following statement appears in the *Journaux intimes* like the first flash of a brooding storm: "Now I am always on the verge of fainting, and today, January 23, 1862, I have had a strange warning: I felt the wings of madness hovering over me." Nevertheless, his activities did not subside. He thanked Sainte-Beuve with an article which appeared in the *Revue Anecdotique:* "Une réforme à l'Académie" (A Reform in the Academy). In March and April he published some old and new poems, articles on Paul de Molènes and *Les Misérables*, and a study which was included in *Curiosités esthétiques* under the title "Peintres et aquafortistes." But his physical and moral weariness was apparent in his letters. His life in Paris, fraught with creditors and cares, was becoming increasingly cumbersome, and he again contemplated moving to Honfleur to live with his mother. Poulet-Malassis' bankruptcy at the end of that year was a new source of disappointment. *Les Fleurs du Mal* and *Paradis artificiels* were withdrawn from circulation and sold at a discount. Some blunders in handling the publication of the *Petits Poëmes en prose* by Arsène Houssaye had caused him much difficulty. He had come to the end of his patience. "My habitual state of mind is one of anger." This anger was directed against himself for the most part. "I am always dissatisfied with myself," he wrote to Champfleury in March, 1863. Three months later he made the some confession to his mother. "You must have racked your brains to find a reason for my not writing; its only real cause was my dissatisfaction with myself." The obsession with his own guilt never ceased to haunt him. When in August 1863 he made plans to go to Belgium for "an excursion of two or three months, for the purpose of visiting the rich private collections of the country and writing a book on his personal impressions," he wanted above all to escape Paris, where his life had become unbearable. It is possible that he was trying to escape from himself also, by a total withdrawal from France. This is perhaps the secret of this voluntary exile that puzzled all his friends as well as his biographers.

This plan met with countless obstacles arising from his own vacillations and "procrastination." The year 1863 went by without his fulfilling it. He published some prose and verse poems, and his fine article on "L'Oeuvre et la vie d'Eugène Delacroix."

"Le Peintre de la vie moderne" finally appeared in November and December, after three years of vicissitudes. His departure for Belgium was put off each week. His plans no longer involved visits to the art galleries there. After August he only entertained the thought of writing articles for *L'Indépendence belge* and of completing his "unfinished books." He also spoke of "public lectures," always planning to return quickly in order to take up residence in Honfleur. In December "readings" at the "Cercle artistique" of Brussels were still on his agenda, but the actual purpose of his trip was "to sell, and for a good price, three volumes of *Variétés*." These successive plans appear to be mere pretexts revolving around his fixed resolution to leave Paris and France, "which he had come to loathe." He finally arrived in Brussels on April 24, 1864 and found a room in the Hôtel du Grand Miroir, where he was to pass the last two years that Fate allotted him for the exercise of his genius.

His genius . . . was it still possible to refer to him thus? His marvelous intelligence had not left him, nor had it lost any of its sharpness and subtlety. However, his creative powers had weakened. He continued to publish poems and translations, but these were simply previously written, heretofore unpublished, pieces. Few of them were really new. He did not stop writing, and composed one of his most significant and stirring texts, the *Journaux intimes*. He had been working on it for a long time. The title does not refer to an actual journal, but to a projected work of several volumes unless it be one only. In April, 1861, he spoke to his mother about an "important book which I have been planning for the past two years: *Mon coeur mis à nu*, into which I will cram all my rages." He proposed a volume to Arsène Houssaye in August, 1862, which would be called *Fusées et suggestions* (a title he had borrowed from Edgar Allan Poe). His notes were later compiled and organized by Poulet-Malassis. Some mention *Fusées*, while others refer to *Suggestions*, or *Mon coeur mis à nu*. Some bear no title whatsoever. Critics have discerned a difference in tone between *Mon coeur mis à nu*, which is angrier and harsher, than *Fusées*. Jacques Crépet, the eminent and meticulous Baudelairean specialist concluded after careful examination that the notes of *Fusées* must have been written between 1855 and 1862, and the others from 1859 to 1866.

These distinctions and specifications are not proven facts. Baudelaire never mentions *two* such books. His proposal of *Fusées et suggestions* to Arsène Houssaye, one year after he had announced *Mon coeur mis à nu* to his mother, is strange. There is not one part of this double volume which could not have fitted both titles without difficulty. If we consider Baudelaire's accustomed hesitations over the titles of his works, it seems likely that he had simply used one title or the other according to his particular mood.

His most direct revelations can be found in the pages of this work. It was not, nor was it meant to be, serene. It was conceived amidst the chaos of a life, which, in spite of its fertility, was constantly haunted by the shadow of failure. It was written by a man whose emotional equilibrium was disintegrating day by day, and whose nervous irritability steadily increased with his circumstances. Baudelaire was to escape this vicious circle only by his death. Some projected articles bear witness to his exasperation and also to his irresolute nature, since they were never completed. In late 1861 or early 1862, he drafted a furious and vindictive text against Villemain, who had treated Chateaubriand unkindly. In a letter to the *Figaro*, written a few days before his departure from France, he lashed out at the organizers of a banquet commemorating the third centennial of the birth of Shakespeare. He accused them of being motivated by political rather than literary considerations. His remarks in the *Journaux intimes* often become violent and virulent protests. "Well then! Yes, this book that I have so much wanted to write will be full of rancor. . . . I will use all my talent to accuse the entire French nation. I have as much need for revenge as a tired man for a bath." We find brutal outbursts against both individuals and groups. More than one contemporary was his target. He identified by name that "Sand woman," whom he described as an "ugly beast, possessed, stupid creature, old simpleton, barrel of trash" and as the "Prudhomme of immorality . . ." He deemed that business "is Satanic by nature." Journalism did not fare better: "It is impossible to read any newspaper, no matter what day, month, or year, without encountering signs of the most hideous human perversity in every line." The man of letters was "the enemy of the world." "Frenchmen are such well domesticated farm-yard animals that they dare not jump over any fences." We know what he thought of women, who are "natural, or, in other words, abominable." Young girls he called "displays of horror, monsters, and murderers of art," and said that they showed "the greatest stupidity coupled with the greatest depravity." It only remained for him to write a "chapter on indestructible, eternal, universal, and ingenious human ferocity."

These are cries of pain rather than of anger. The overall impression conveyed by this book is one of metaphysical anguish and of a most intense kind of spiritual aspiration, a fervent, humble, and sincere faith. "My humiliations have been favors from God." In such instances we penetrate to the depth of Baudelaire's character. This man, who was proud by reputation, who wrote to the editor of a magazine that he had considered himself infallible since childhood, was a modest person in the hidden reaches of his being, devoid of self-confidence, and in need of support and encouragement. He was a person who recited his prayers before God with childish simplicity.

He himself relates a curious and touching incident which sums up his character. He related to Nadar that he became embroiled in a fight with a Belgian: "It is unbelievable, is it not? That I should fight with anyone is absurd. And what was even more preposterous yet was that I was completely wrong. When my spirit of fairness got the better of me, I ran after the man in order to apologize. But I could not find him."

Baudelaire had spent hardly two months in Belgium when he began to talk of sending a series of "Lettres belges" (Letters from Belgium) to the *Figaro*, under a pseudonym. He would subsequently sell them as a book. From its very beginning this book had the makings of one of the most ferocious criticisms ever formulated against an entire nation. The Belgians did not take him seriously, and rightfully so. In spite of appearances, the fury which emanates from these pages was not caused by anything Belgian. It was simply that it was to Belgium that circumstances had led him, that his proposed lectures turned out to be a fiasco. He received only a minor income from them. His stay in Belgium became divested of all sense, though he felt himself incapable of terminating this exile. He was, as he wrote in his prose poem, "unhappy with everything and dissatisfied with himself."

He found in the Belgians the same qualities which had irritated him so much in his own countrymen. Increasing pain rendered him more and more vulnerable, and more and more incapable of controlling his fits of temper. Here is the explanation of the book he gave to Ancelle: "The purpose of this satyric (*sic*) book is the mockery of all that people call 'progress' and which I myself call 'the paganism of the imbeciles'—and the proof of the sovereignty of God." He worked on this book, titled *Pauvre Belgique,* with dogged persistence, doing research on the history, the institutions, and even the commerce and industry of the country. A mass of notes went into the composition of the three hundred and sixty page manuscript. Only those pages dealing with works of art, paintings, and monuments are of any interest at all to us. Baudelaire manifested his admiration for the Jesuit style of architecture, and for that church in Namur in particular where he was to suffer his first collapse: "*Saint-Loup.* A handsome and sinister marvel. . . . The interior of a catafalque trimmed with black, crimson, and silver." The rest of this enormous repository of invective makes boring reading, and adds nothing to its author's glory.

The shortcomings of this work could be explained by the rapid progress of his illness. Hardly had he arrived in Belgium when he began to suffer attacks, which sometimes lasted several weeks and which became increasingly painful. The doctors whom he consulted prescribed sedatives and had no great knowledge of the cause of his malady. They guessed hysteria. * Baudelaire had no illusions about the inanity of this diagnosis: "In good French, it means I give up." He did not take care of himself properly, and often lacked the means to buy drugs. The attacks became more acute, and were accompanied by unbearable headaches. "This is the set pattern: I feel perfectly fine, I have not eaten anything, and suddenly, without any forewarning or apparent cause I feel light, distracted, and faint; and then a hideous pain in my head. I must absolutely collapse, unless I am already lying on my back at the time.—Then a cold

* (Today we are fairly certain that the cause was syphilis, though we have no definite proof.)

sweat, vomiting, and a prolonged daze." Crazed by suffering toward the end, he turned to brandy in an effort to find moments of peace and oblivion through intoxication.

Though this physical deterioration weakened his creative genius, his lucidity remained nevertheless unimpaired. Though his distaste for society culminated in an abiding fury, his capacity for affection and friendship seemed to increase in proportion. He was full of tenderness towards his mother, was anxious about her most minor indispositions, and hoped only that he would be capable of mending his faults and of taking up life with her. Ancelle, the legal advisor and administrator of his income, who had been his pet aversion for a long time, now became "his dear friend" and "his dear Ancelle." He did not stop thanking him for "all the affection that he had always shown him," for his dedication and kind services. He expressed his feelings in his own peculiar way: "Do not deprive me of the only friend whom I could abuse!"

His spirituality was strengthened in its orthodoxy. He was no longer satisfied with asking his mother and his friends to pray for him, as he had done on more than one occasion; he himself started praying. The fact is mentioned in the *Journaux intimes,* and in this letter to Madame Paul Meurice: "I am praying for your happiness (as I pray for all those whom I love)." He told his mother of his plans for reform and work, and of his intention to do all within his power to make her happy. His thoughts turned to God: "Sometimes I think with a shudder that God could take this possibility away from me. . . . How many times has God already given me fifteen more months on credit!"

He felt the presence of Evil in the heart of man, and, above all, in his own heart: "Monsieur Baudelaire has the necessary genius for studying crime within his own heart." This avowal is not new. The redemptive value of suffering was one of his oldest ideas, one which served as a supporting element for the theme of *Les Fleurs du Mal.* He did not hesitate to express it anew, in an extreme form. "I deem it good that innocence should suffer." One of his greatest sources of irritation against the Belgians was their materialism, atheism, and anti-clericalism.

His illness spared his admirable critical intelligence and his love for poetry and letters. "Literature comes before everything, before my stomach, my pleasure, and my mother." His preferences did not waver; he re-read Lucain and Chateaubriand, whom he still intended to avenge "for the insults showered upon him by the young riff-raff of today." He planned to make a new translation of Maturin's *Bertram.* He considered doing a second translation of his *Melmoth.* His fidelity towards Sainte-Beuve was not shaken, and he intended to write an article entitled "Sainte-Beuve, ou *Joseph Delorme* jugé par l'auteur des *Fleurs du mal.*" For him, *Joseph Delorme* represented "the *Flowers of Evil* in the bud." Though he admired and respected Sainte-Beuve, the awareness of his own genius allowed Baudelaire to judge him with the noble candor of a master: "In certain portions of *Joseph Delorme* I find too many lutes, lyres, harps, and Jehovahs. It mars the Parisian poems. And still you had come to destroy all that."

He needed some pluck not to lose confidence in himself, for selling his works had never been so difficult. Poulet-Malassis' bankruptcy left him in a dramatic position. Poulet-Malassis no longer had the right to publish Baudelaire's work. But Baudelaire was incapable of buying back "the exclusive rights to publication of his work in any form, both published and unpublished" which he had granted to Poulet-Malassis in 1862. Baudelaire further complicated his troubles when, in spite of this previous contract, he offered *Les Fleurs du Mal* and *Petits Poëmes en prose* to Hetzel. His mother and Ancelle helped to extricate him from this situation. The case was settled in July, 1865. At this time, he attempted to find a new publisher. He spent about ten days in France, at Honfleur and in Paris, in order to terminate this affair. On this occasion, Catulle Mendès encountered him at the Gare du Nord, completely bewildered, and, having taken him to his flat, heard his dispirited avowal: "The sum total of my life's savings: fifteen thousand eight hundred ninety-two francs and sixty centimes!" Mendès has possibly exaggerated this incident somewhat. But it is quite true that Baudelaire's distress was acute.

In anticipation of the conclusion of his law case, Baudelaire had commissioned various intermediaries to offer six available volumes to publishers. These included *Pauvre Belgique* and

Edgar Allan Poe's *Histoires grotesques et sérieuses.* The latter was put up for sale by Michel Levy on March 16, 1865. Five volumes were offered to Garnier. They eliminated *Pauvre Belgique* immediately. The transaction was carried on amidst countless difficulties caused by misunderstanding and distance. After months of negotiation, they came to a negative decision. One reason for their refusal was that *Les Fleurs du Mal* was "a forgotten book." This made Baudelaire wince. "This is really idotic. The book is constantly in demand. Perhaps people will begin to understand it in a few years." The exhausting and discouraging discussions were resumed with other publishers. His one satisfaction lay in *Les Épaves,* printed secretly by Poulet-Malassis. It contained old and new poems, together with the condemned pieces. This was a clandestine edition, officially denied by Baudelaire, and one which was banned in France.

As his days were drawing to a close, "in the shadows of oblivion," fame slowly appeared on the horizon, and its first echoes reached the exile. The poets of the younger generation looked upon him with respect. Leon Cladel, Catulle Mendès, and Villiers de l'Isle Adam paid him tributes full of enthusiastic admiration. His reputation extended beyond national boundaries. "Sometimes I receive from distant places, and from people unknown to me, letters of sympathy which I find very touching, but which do not console me in my despicable misery and humiliating condition, nor do they alleviate my vices." A Frenchman wrote to him from London, having become acquainted with his works "through a young friend, Monsieur Stéphane Mallarmé." Another person sent him a remarkable piece of criticism concerning *Les Fleurs du Mal* from Bucharest. In 1862, Swinburne had written a fine article which was published in *The Spectator.* In early 1866, Catulle Mendès, who had solicited Baudelaire's support for *Lectures poétiques* three years before, asked him to collaborate in *Le Parnasse Contemporain.* At the same time, Baudelaire heard of the publication, in November and December, 1865, of the first extended study of his work. It was written by a young poet both enthusiastic and unknown: Paul Verlaine. Sainte-Beuve gave him the news, and told him at the same time that he was considered as a master by the new School: "Were you here, you would become, whether you wanted to or not, an authority, an oracle, and an advisor."

The limelight caused him to blink his eyes, long accustomed to obscurity. He became suspicious and tried to step back. He was worried and pleased at the same time. "These youngsters have talent," he remarked in a letter to his mother, "but also what foolishness! What extremes and youthful infatuations! Here and there I have come upon imitations and alarming tendencies. I can imagine no one more indiscreet than an imitator, and I like nothing better than to be left alone. But that is impossible; it seems that the *Baudelairean School* exists."

He wrote these lines on March 5, 1866. On March 18, he visited the church of Saint-Loup at Namur, which had taken his fancy because of its "Jesuitic" style. He was accompanied by Félicien Rops and Poulet-Malassis, two friends who had helped him most to bear up under his exile. He suffered a fainting spell which left him exhausted. A more serious attack followed two days later; it left him paralyzed. He was unable to use his hands. He was forced to dictate his letters. He nevertheless remained lucid. He gave extremely precise instructions to Catulle Mendès, who was preparing to publish the "Nouvelles Fleurs du Mal" (New Flowers of Evil) in his *Parnasse Contemporain.* He even made specifications about the typography: "The title should be written in such a way that *Fleurs du Mal* is distinct from the word *Nouvelles.*" He thanked his old friend, Prarond, who had just sent him a volume of poetry, congratulating him and pointing out a wrong scansion at the same time. He sent three perfectly coherent letters on March 30: he intended to visit five or six more towns in connection with his book on Belgium, which he had not stopped writing. He was struck by hemiplegia on the same day, with concomitant softening of the brain.

The man who remained no longer resembled Baudelaire. He spent a few months in a clinic in Brussels and was later transferred to his hotel. He was finally transported to Paris on July 2, and placed in a mental home. This wretched existence continued for one year, interspersed from time to time by rare moments of lucidity, when his expressionless face would light up at the sight of a friend, or when his abiding affection for

Wagner caused him to respond to the strains of his music. He was finally liberated on August 31, 1867, and departed for those "wonders beyond the grave, on which his poetry had tried to cast a glimmer of light."

His funeral attracted only about a hundred men of letters. Over his grave, in the cemetery of Montparnasse, the judgment of posterity was pronounced for the first time by Banville: "The author of *Les Fleurs du Mal* was not merely a talented poet, but a man of genius. . . ."

Conclusion

THIS GENIUS was not then recognized by many. Half a century was to pass before it was unanimously acknowledged. Once Baudelaire's works became public property in 1917, the editions began to multiply and diffuse his name. In 1922, Jacques Crépet set a unique example in the history of literature, by embarking on the path forged by his father, and undertaking his monumental edition of Baudelaire's complete works. The last volumes were published only after Crépet's death, with the help of Monsieur Pichois. Baudelaire had remained for too long a time the idol of a select few.

The "misunderstanding" which Baudelaire had lamented in 1857 continued to prevail among his most vociferous admirers. Baudelaire remained primarily the poet of carrion and other morbid subjects for many of his followers, as well as for his enemies. We will not dwell upon the illegitimate progeny which still issues from him. The most notorious example of it is Maurice Rollinat, a native of Berry, who abandoned his inherent pastoral traditions in order to write *Les Névroses.*

Some exponents of the authentic Baudelairean heritage have also neglected the essentials. Trained ears could not disregard his peculiar musicality. If one agrees with Valéry that the originality of the symbolists lay in their intention to "reinstate music to its rightful place," it is evident that Baudelaire was their master. His first disciple, Verlaine, was much indebted to him for the techniques of musicality. We are not here questioning Verlaine's originality. His genius had only slight affinities with Baudelaire's. He appropriated only those elements of Baudelaire's work which specifically corresponded to his own temperament. Verlaine's musicality is studied and subtle. One can describe him with the same words that Flaubert had used in connection with *Les Fleurs du Mal*: "penetrating as the London fog," but not with the end of the sentence: "hard as marble." The resources of versification and language which were at Verlaine's disposal affect our sensitivity rather than our souls. He does indeed penetrate our spirit in his best moments, but this is achieved by simply communicating his own feelings, and not, as in Baudelaire's case, by stirring ours to their very depths. Both his method and content are much more superficial than Baudelaire's.

Baudelaire's other disciple, Mallarmé, arrived at a better understanding of his technique. He made use of the internal powers of language in his poetry and in his prose. He set an immensely ambitious goal for poetry—"the orphic explanation of the earth." His work achieved a poetic intensity which was never equalled before him. It is "concentrated" in the strict sense of that word, and exists for its own sake. It is, therefore, reminiscent of Art for Art's Sake, and not completely within the Baudelairean heritage.

Rimbaud also grasped all the new implications of Baudelaire's concept of poetic language. His *Saison en Enfer* (Season in Hell), as well as his *Illuminations*, bears an immediate relationship to Baudelaire's art. They constitute its logical development.

Baudelaire's prose and verse poems were the basis for the dislocation and simplification effected by Verlaine in his poetry. This was the starting point of a complete break with the old concepts of versification; it was, in a sense, free verse—that is to say, the very elimination of verse. The "liberation" of modern poetry is due to the free use of the interior poetic powers of language. This permits an abolition of the more obvious technical means. In French poetry, it was Baudelaire who first used this method in *Les Fleurs du Mal* and *Le Spleen de Paris*.

Though Baudelaire did not invent the Theory of Correspondences, he nevertheless can be credited with having extended its meaning to poetry. But how many poets endow these mysterious Correspondences with the significance which Baudelaire considered to be their unique validity?

Rimbaud is Baudelaire's heir in the most profound sense. For him, as for Baudelaire, poetry was not a distraction, but action, and "a way of life," as Tristan Tzara calls it. Its function consisted not in expressing sadness or gaiety, but in presenting the problems of the human condition and destiny to the reader. At about the same time as Rimbaud, Lautréamont set forth an identical conception of poetry in his *Chants de Maldoror* (Songs of Maldoror). They are the direct descendants of Baudelaire. This lineage later included Alfred Jarry and the surrealists. If their poetry seems violent for the most part, it is because it was not enough for it simply to exist. They all want their work to act upon the reader. As early as 1857, a perspicacious critic said of *Les Fleurs du Mal*: "We are not charmed, but violently shaken."

The transformation of the very notion of poetry was certainly not the result of Baudelaire's influence alone. The German Romantics, Gérard de Nerval, and the Jeune-France had already made steps in this direction. But Baudelaire focused all these faint flickers into a beam of dazzling light. His work was the decisive influence. He claims an incomparably wider and more far-reaching effect on foreign literature than anyone else.

Even today, though poetic production on the whole conforms to his aesthetic principles, total unanimity does not exist. But regardless of future developments, a backward step is no longer possible. In the hierarchy of values, Baudelaire's inspiration occupies a high place. His work affected the course of Poetry more radically than anyone else in its entire history.

BIBLIOGRAPHICAL NOTES

I. CHRONOLOGICAL TABLE OF BOOKS, POEMS, TRANSLATIONS, AND ARTICLES PUBLISHED BY BAUDELAIRE

The titles of volumes and brochures are printed in italics; those of articles which appeared in periodicals are printed with quotation marks; those of both prose and verse poems are printed in boldface type. The translations from the works of Edgar Allan Poe have their titles enclosed in quotation marks; the original title follows in parentheses except when it is the same as the title used in translation. The signature which appeared with the work is mentioned, if it is other than "Charles Baudelaire." This table does not include reprints, except in a few inevitable cases.

The initials at the end of each entry refer to the volumes of the Conard edition in which the work may be found. The abbreviations used are as follows:

FM	*Les Fleurs du Mal*
PPP	*Petits poëmes en prose, Le Jeune Enchanteur*
PA	*Les Paradis artificiels, La Fanfarlo*
CE	*Curiosités esthétiques*
AR	*L'Art romantique*
OP	*Œuvres posthumes*, 3 vol.
CG	*Correspondance générale*, 6 vol.
HE	*Histoires extraordinaires*
NHE	*Nouvelles Histoires extraordinaires*
HGS	*Histoires grotesques et sérieuses*

AGP *Les Aventures d'Arthur Gordon Pym*
E *Eurêka, La Genèse d'un poëme, Le Corbeau*

1844

Probably collaborated in *Mystères galans des théâtres de Paris,* (Gallant Mysteries in the Theatres of Paris), Cazel, Paris, 1844. OP, I

1845

First half of May: *Salon de 1845,* signed Baudelaire-Dufaÿs, Jules Labitte, Paris, 1845, 72pp. CE

May 25: **A une Créole [A une dame Créole]** (To a Creole; also titled To a Creole Lady), signed Baudelaire-Dufaÿs, *L'Artiste.* FM

November 4: "Les Contes Normands et Historiettes baguenaudières, par Jean de Falaise" (Norman Tales and Trifling Ancedotes, by Jean de Falaise), anonymous review, *Le Corsaire-Satan.* OP, I

November 25: "Sapho" (Sappho), anonymous. Fragment of a tragedy fictitiously attributed to Arsène Houssaye, written in collaboration with Banville, Pierre Dupont, and Vitu, *Le Corsaire-Satan.* OP, I

1846

January 21: "Le Musée classique du Bazar Bonne-Nouvelle" (The Classic Museum of the Bonne-Nouvelle Bazaar), signed Baudelaire-Dufaÿs, *Le Corsaire-Satan.* CE

February 3: "Promethée délivré, par L. de Senneville" (Prometheus Delivered, by L. de Senneville), followed by a few lines on "Le Siècle, épître à Chateaubriand, par Bathild Bouniol" (The Century, a Letter to Chateaubriand, by Bathild Bouniol), reviews signed Baudelaire-Dufays, *Le Corsaire-Satan.* OP, I

February 20, 21, and 22: "Le Jeune Enchanteur" (The Young Magician), short story signed Baudelaire-Dufays, *L'Esprit public.* PPP

March 3: "Choix de maximes consolantes sur l'amour" (A Selection of Comforting Maxims about Love), signed Baudelaire-Dufays, *Le Corsaire-Satan.* OP, II

April 15: "Conseils aux jeunes littérateurs" (Advice to Young Men of Letters), signed Baudelaire-Dufays, *L'Esprit public.* AR

April: *Le Salon caricatural* (The Salon of Caricature), anonymous, in collaboration with Banville and Vitu. (Baudelaire is supposed to have written the Prologue, and a few rhyming mottoes.) Charpentier, Paris, 32pp. OP, II

May: *Salon de 1846*, signed Baudelaire-Dufays, Michael Lévy Bros., Paris, 1846, 132pp. CE

September 6: **L'Impénitent [Don Juan aux Enfers]** (The Impenitent; also titled Don Juan in Hell), signed Baudelaire-Dufays, *L'Artiste.* FM

December 13: **A une Indienne [A une Malabaraise]** (To an Indian Girl; also titled To a Malabar Girl), signed Pierre de Fayis, *L'Artiste.* FM

From September 15, 1846 to March 28, 1847: "Causeries" (Chats), anonymous, in collaboration with Banville and Vitu, *Le Tintamarre.* OP, I

1847

January: "La Fanfarlo," signed Charles Defayis, *Bulletin de la Société des gens de lettres.* PA

November 14: **Les Chats** (The Cats), anonymous, in a serial by Champfleury, *Le Corsaire.* FM

1848

January 18: "Les Contes de Champfleury, Chien-Caillou, Pauvre Trompette, Feu Miette" (The Stories of Champfleury: The Dog Flint, The Poor Trumpet, and The Particle of Fire), *Le Corsaire.* OP, I

February 27 and March 1: Collaboration on two issues of *Le Salut Public.* OP, I

April 10 to June 6: Collaboration on *La Tribune Nationale.*

(See Jules Mouquet and W. T. Bandy, *Baudelaire en 1848, La Tribune Nationale*, Emile-Paul, Paris, 1946.)

July 15: "Révélation Magnétique" (Translation of "Mesmeric Revelation"), preceded by a Notice, *La Liberté du Peuple.* HE

November: **Le Vin de l'assassin** (The Wine of the Assassin), *L'Echo des marchands de vin,* No. 2. FM

1850

June: **Châtiment de l'orgueil** (The Punishment of Pride), and **Le Vin des honnêtes gens** [**L'Ame du vin**] (The Honest Man's Wine; also titled The Soul of Wine), *Le Magasin des Familles.* FM

July: **Lesbos,** in *Les Poëtes de l'amour,* a selection of French verse with an introduction by Julian Lemer, Paris, 1850. FM

"Biographie des excentriques" (Biography of Eccentrics), anonymous (attribution doubtful), *La République du Peuple, Almanach démocratique pour 1851.* OP, II

1851

March 7, 8, 11, and 12: "Du Vin et du Hachich" [*Sic*] (Concerning Wine and Hashish), *Le Messager de l'Assemblée.* PA

April 9: under the collective title of "Les Limbes" (Limbo): **Le Spleen** [**Pluviôse irrité**] (Spleen; also titled Angry Pluviôse), **Le mauvais Moine** (The Wicked Monk), **L'Idéal** (The Ideal), **Le Spleen** [**Le Mort joyeux**] (Spleen; also titled The Happy Dead Man), reprint of **Les Chats** (The Cats), **La Mort des artistes** (The Death of Artists), **La Mort des amants** (The Death of Lovers), **Le Tonneau de la haine** (The Cask of Hate), **La Béatrix** [**De profundis clamavi**], **Le Spleen** [**La Cloche fêlée**] (Spleen; later called The Cracked Bell), and **Les Hiboux** (The Owls), *Le Messager de l'Assemblée.* FM

November 27: "Les drames et les romans honnêtes" (Gentile Plays and Dramas), *La Semaine théâtrale.* AR

"Notice sur Pierre Dupont" (Short note on Pierre Dupont) at the beginning of the collection *Chants et chansons,* Vol. 20.

1852

January 22: "L'École païenne" (The Pagan School), *La Semaine théâtrale.* AR

February 1: **Les deux Crépuscules [Le Crépuscule du matin, Le Crépuscule du soir]** (The Two Twilights; also titled separately Morning Twilight and Evening Twilight), *La Semaine théâtrale.* FM

March and April: "Edgar Allan Poe, sa vie et ses ouvrages" (Edgar Allan Poe, His Life and Work), *Revue de Paris.* OP, I

April 17: "Bérénice" (translation), preceded by an anonymous Notice, *L'Illustration.* NHE

October: **Le Reniement de saint Pierre** (The Denial of Saint Peter), **L'Homme libre et la mer [L'Homme et la mer]** (The Free Man and the Sea; also titled Man and the Sea), *Revue de Paris.* FM

October: "Le Puits et la pendule" (translation of "The Pit and the Pendulum"), *Revue de Paris.* NHE

October: "Philosophie d'ameublement" (translation of "Philosophy of Furniture"), *Le Magasin des Familles.* HGS

December 11: "Une Aventure dans les Montagnes Rocheuses"; also titled "Les Souvenirs de M. Auguste Bedloe" (translation of "A Tale of the Ragged Mountains"), *L'Illustration.* HE

1853

February 4: "Le Coeur Révélateur" (translation of "The Tell-Tale Heart"), *Paris Journal.* NHE

March 1: "Le Corbeau" (translation of "The Raven"), *L'Artiste.* E

April 17: "Morale du Joujou (Ethics of Toys), *Le Monde littéraire.* AR

November 13 and 14: "Le Chat noir" (translation of "The Black Cat"), *Paris.* NHE

November 14 and 15: "Morella" (translation), *Paris.* HE

1854

July 25: "A Madame Maria Clemm, à Milford (Connecticut)" (To Mrs. Maria Clemm in Milford, Connecticut), at the beginning of "Une Aventure dans les Montagnes Rocheuses" (translation of "A Tale of the Ragged Mountains"), *Le Pays.* HE

July 27: "Entretien d'Eiros avec Charmion"; also titled "Conversation d'Eiros avec Charmion" (translation of "The Conversation of Eiros and Charmion"), *Le Pays.* NHE

July 28: "L'Homme Caméléopard ou quatre bêtes en une"; also titled "Quatre bêtes en une" (translation of "Four Beasts in One; The Homo-Camelopard"), *Le Pays.* NHE

August 5: "Puissance de la Parole" (translation of "The Power of Words"), and "L'Ombre" (translation of "Shadow—A Parable"), *Le Pays.* NHE

September 13: "La Barrique d'Amontillado" (translation of "The Cask of Amontillado"), *Le Pays.* NHE

September 14: "Le Démon de la perversité" (translation of "The Imp of the Perverse"), *Le Pays.* NHE

September 17: "Metzengerstein" (translation), *Le Pays.* HE

September 20: "Le Diable dans le Beffroi" (translation of "The Devil in the Belfrey"), *Le Pays.* HE

September 20 and 26: "Mort ou Vivant? Cas de M. Valdemar"; also titled "La Vérité sur le cas de M. Valdemar" (translation of "The Facts in the Case of M. Valdemar"), *Le Pays.* HE

December 11 and 12: "Petite discussion avec une momie (translation of "Some Words with a Mummy"), *Le Pays.* NHE

1855

January 15: **Que diras-tu ce soir, pauvre âme solitaire . . .** (What Will You Say Tonight, My Poor, Lonely Soul?), quoted without crediting Baudelaire, in "L'Assassinat du Pont-Rouge" (The Murder at Pont-Rouge) by Charles Barbara, in *Revue de Paris.* FM

January 21 and 22: "Manuscrit trouvé dans une bouteille" (translation of "MS. Found in a Bottle"), *Le Pays.* HE

January 22 and 23: "Le Colloque de Monos et d'Una" (translation of "The Colloquy of Monos and Una"), *Le Pays.* NHE

January 23, 26, and 27: "Le Roi Peste" (translation of "King Pest"), *Le Pays.* NHE

January 27 and 28: "L'Homme des foules" (translation of "The Man of the Crowd"), *Le Pays.* NHE

January 28: "Le Portrait ovale" (translation of "The Oval Portrait"), *Le Pays.* NHE

January 28 and 30: "L'Ile de la fée" (translation of "The Island of the Fay"), *Le Pays.* NHE

January 31, February 2 and 3: "Le Canard au ballon" (translation of "The Balloon Hoax"), *Le Pays.* HE

February 3 and 4: "Ligeia" (translation), *Le Pays.* HE

February 5, 6, and 7: "Une Descente dans le Maelstrom" (translation of "A Descent into the Maelstrom"), *Le Pays.* HE

February 7, 9, and 13: "La Chute de la maison Usher" (translation of "The Fall of the House of Usher"), *Le Pays.* NHE

February 14, 15, 18, and 19: "William Wilson" (translation), *Le Pays.* NHE

February 19 and 22: "Être un Lion, conte moral"; also titled "Lionnerie" (translation of "Lionizing"), *Le Pays.* NHE

February 22: "Le Silence"; later titled "Silence" (translation of "Silence—A Fable"), *Le Pays.* NHE

February 22 and 23: "Le Masque de la mort rouge" (translation of "The Masque of the Red Death"), *Le Pays.* NHE

February 23, 24, and 25: "Hop-Frog" (translation), *Le Pays.* NHE

February 25 and 26; March 1, 2, 3, 5, 6, and 7: "Facultés divinatoires d'Auguste Dupin, I"; also titled "Double assassinat dans la rue Morgue" (translation of "The Murders in the Rue Morgue"), *Le Pays.* HE

March 7, 8, 12, and 14: "Facultés divinatoires d'Auguste Dupin, II"; also titled "La Lettre volée" (translation of "The Purloined Letter"), *Le Pays.* HE

March 14, 15, 16, 22, 27, 31; April 1, 2, 14, 17, and 20: "Aventures sans pareille d'un certain Hans Pfaall" (translation of "The Unparalleled Adventures of One Hans Pfaall"), *Le Pays.* HE

May 26 and June 3: "Exposition Universelle, 1855," Parts I and III, *Le Pays.* CE

May: Under the collective title of "Les deux Crépuscules" (The Two Twilights): a letter "A Fernand Desnoyers" (To Fernand Desnoyers), now in CG, I; and, after a reprint of **Crépuscule du matin** (Morning Twilight) and **Crépuscule du soir** (Evening Twilight) in verse—now in FM—there follow **Le Crépuscule du soir** and **La Solitude** (Solitude) as prose poems, now in PPP. The foregoing appeared in *Fountainebleau, Hommage à Denecourt,* Hachette, Paris, 1855.

June 1: Under the collective title "Les Fleurs du Mal," and with an epigraph by Agrippa d'Aubigné, 18 poems: **Au lecteur** (To the Reader), **Réversibilité** (Reversibility), reprint of **Le Tonneau de la haine** (The Cask of Hate), **La Confession** (Confession), **L'Aube Spirituelle** (Spiritual Dawn), **La Volupté** [**La Destruction**] (Pleasure; also titled Destruction), **Voyage à Cythère** (Voyage to Cytherea), **A la Belle aux cheveux d'or** [**L'Irréparable**] (To the Beautiful Woman with Golden Hair; also titled The Irreparable), **L'Invitation au voyage** (Invitation to a Journey), **Moesta et errabunda** (Sad and Restless), reprint of **La Cloche** [La Cloche fêlée] (The Bell; later called The Cracked Bell), **L'Ennemi** (The Enemy), **La Vie antérieure** (A Former Life), reprint of **Le Spleen** [**De profundis clamavi**] (Spleen; later titled Out of the Depths), **Remords posthume** (The Remorse of the Dead), **Le Guignon** (Bad Luck), **La Béatrice** [**Le Vampire**] (Beatrice; also titled The Vampire), **L'Amour et le crâne** (**d'après une vieille gravure**) (Love and the Skull: After an Old Engraving), *Revue des Deux Mondes.* FM

July 8: "De l'Essence du Rire et généralement du comique dans les arts plastiques" (The Essence of Laughter, and More Especially of the Comic, in the Plastic Arts), *Le Portefeuille.* (A short fragment of this article had been previously quoted in *Contes d'automne* (Tales of Autumn) by Champfleury, Victor Lecou, Paris, 1854, pp. 296–97.) CE

August 12: "Exposition Universelle, 1855," Part II, *Le Portefeuille.* CE

"Philibert Rouvière," article in *Nouvelle Galérie des artistes dramatiques vivants,* 61st issue, Librairie théâtrale, Paris, no date. (1855).

1856

February 25: Fragment of "Edgar Poe, sa vie et ses ouvrages" (Edgar Poe: His Life and Works), *Le Pays.* HE

March 12: *Histoires extraordinaires* (Tales of the Grotesque; collection of translated short stories), Michel Lévy, Paris, 1856, 331pp. It included one previously unpublished story, "Le Scarabée d'or" (translation of "The Gold Bug"). HE

1857

February 25 to April 18: "La Relation d'Arthur Gordon Pym"; later titled "Les Aventures d'Arthur Gordon Pym" (translation of "Narrative of A. Gordon Pym"), *Le Moniteur Universel.* AGP

Early part of March: *Nouvelles Histoires Extraordinaires* (More Tales of the Grotesque; translations of short stories), Michel Lévy, Paris, 1857, 288pp. It contained the previously unpublished article "Notes nouvelles sur Edgar Poe" (New Notes on Edgar Poe). NHE

April 20: **La Beauté** (Beauty), **La Géante** (The Giantess), **Le Flambeau vivant** (The Living Torch), **Harmonie du soir** (Evening Harmony), **Le Flacon** (The Flask), **Le Poison** (Poison), **Tout entière** (The Whole), **Sonnet [Avec ses vêtements ondoyants et nacrés . . .]** (Sonnet: With her swaying robes, covered with mother-of-pearl . . .), **Sonnet [Je te donne ces vers afin que si mon nom . . .]** (Sonnet: I give you these verses . . .), *Revue Française.* FM

May 10: **L'Héautontimorouménos, L'Irrémédiable** (The Irremediable), **Franciscae meae laudes** (In Praise of My Francesca), *L'Artiste.* FM

June 25: *Les Fleurs du Mal* (The Flowers of Evil), Poulet-Malassis and de Broise, Paris, 1857, 256pp.

August 24: Under the overall title of "Poëmes nocturnes"

(Night Poems) the following poems in prose: reprint of "**Le Crépuscule du soir** (Evening Twilight), reprint of **La Solitude** (Solitude), **Les Projets** (Projects), **L'Horloge** (The Clock), **La Chevelure** (Her Hair), **L'Invitation au voyage** (Invitation to a Journey), *Le Présent.* PPP

August: *Articles justificatifs pour Charles Baudelaire, auteur des Fleurs du Mal* (Articles in Defense of Charles Baudelaire, author of *The Flowers of Evil*), Dondey-Dupré, Paris, 1857, 33pp. Preface by Baudelaire. OP, II

October 1: "Quelques caricaturistes français" (Several French Caricaturists), *Le Présent.* CE

October 15: "Quelques caricaturistes étrangers" (Several Foreign Caricaturists), *Le Présent.* CE

October 18: "Monsieur Gustave Flaubert.—Madame Bovary.—La Tentation de saint Antoine." ["Madame Bovary, par Gustave Flaubert"] (Gustave Flaubert, Madame Bovary, and The Temptation of Saint Anthony; also titled Madame Bovary, by Gustave Flaubert), *L'Artiste.* AR

November 15: **Paysage [Paysage parisien]** (Landscape; also titled Parisian Landscape), reprint of **A une Malarbaraise** (To a Malabar Girl), **Hymne** (Hymn), **Une Gravure de Mortimer [Une Gravure fantastique]** (An Engraving by Mortimer; later titled A Fantastic Engraving), **La Rançon** (The Ransom), *Le Présent.* FM

1858

May: Reprint of *Aventures d'Arthur Gordon Pym* (translation of "Narrative of A. Gordon Pym") Michel Lévy, Paris, 1858, 280pp. AGP

June 10: Letter "Au directeur du Figaro" (To the Editor of the *Figaro*), *Figaro.* CG, II

September 19: **Duellum** (The Duel), *L'Artiste.* FM

September 30: "Le Poëme du Haschisch" (Hashish Poem), *Revue Contemporaine.* PA

1859

January 9: "La double vie, par Charles Asselineau" (The Double Life, by Charles Asselineau), review, *L'Artiste.* AR

January 20: **Le Goût du néant** (The Taste of Nothingness), **Le Possédé** (The Possessed), *Revue Française*. FM

March 10: "Eleonora" (translation), *Revue Française*. HGS

March 13: "Théophile Gautier," article, *L'Artiste*. AR

March 15: **Danse macabre** (Dance of Death), *Revue Contemporaine*. FM

March 20: "Un événement à Jérusalem" (translation of "A Tale of Jerusalem"), *Revue Française*. HGS

April 10: **Sisina** (Sisina), **Le Voyage** (The Journey), **L'Albatros** (The Albatross), *Revue Française*. FM

April 20: "La Genèse d'un poëme" (translation of "The Philosophy of Composition"), *Revue Française*. E

May 20: **La Chevelure** (Her Hair), verse, *Revue Française*. FM

June 10, 20, and July 20: "Lettres à M. le Directeur de la *Revue Française* sur le Salon de 1859" ["Salon de 1859"] (Letters to the Editor of the *Revue Française* on the Salon of 1859; also titled the Salon of 1859), *Revue Française*. CE

November: Reprint of *Théophile Gautier, Notice littéraire précédée d'une lettre de Victor Hugo* (Théophile Gautier, a review, preceded by a letter by Victor Hugo), Poulet-Malassis & de Broise, Paris, 1859, 68pp. AR

November 30: **Sonnet d'automne** (Autumn Sonnet), **Chant d'automne** (Autumn Song), **Le Masque** (The Mask), *Revue Contemporaine*. FM

October 1859 to January 1860: "Eurêka, poëme en prose, ou Essai sur l'univers matériel et spirituel" (unfinished translation of "Eureka"), *Revue Internationale mensuelle* (Geneva). E

1860

January 15, 31: "Un Mangeur d'opium" (An Opium Eater), *Revue Contemporaine*. PA

January 22: **Le Squelette Laboureur** (The Ploughing Skeleton), **A une Madone** (To a Madonna), **Le Cygne** (The Swan), *La Causerie*. FM

February 17: "L'Ange du Bizarre" (translation of "The Angel of the Odd"), *La Presse.* HGS

May 15: **Rêve parisien** (Parisian Dream), **L'Amour du mensonge** (The Love of Lying), **Le Rêve d'un curieux** (The Dream of a Curious Man), **Semper eadem** (Always the Same), **Obsession** (Obsession), *Revue Contemporaine.* FM.

May: *Les Paradis artificiels. Opium et Haschisch* (Artificial Heavens: Opium and Hashish), Poulet-Malassis & de Broise, Paris, 1860, 304pp.

October 15: **Horreur sympathique** (Sympathetic Horror), **Les Aveugles** (The Blind), **Alchimie de la douleur** (The Alchemy of Pain), **A une passante** (To a Passing Woman), **Un Fantôme** (A Phantom), **Chanson d'après-midi** (Song of the Afternoon), **Hymne à la Beauté** (Hymn to Beauty), **L'Horloge** (The Clock) in verse, *L'Artiste.* FM

1861

First week in February: *Les Fleurs du Mal,* second edition, enlarged with thirty-five new poems, Paulet-Malassis & de Broise, Paris, 1861, 319pp.

February 28: **La Voix** (The Voice), **Le Calumet de paix (imité de Longfellow)** (The Peace-Pipe: an Imitation of Longfellow), *Revue Contemporaine.* FM

April 1: "Richard Wagner" ["Richard Wagner et Tannhäuser à Paris"] (Richard Wagner; also titled Richard Wagner and Tannhäuser in Paris), *Revue Européenne.* AR

End of April: Reprint of *Richard Wagner et Tannhäuser à Paris,* Dentu, Paris, 1861, 70pp. Same text as article of April 1, followed by "Encore quelques mots" (A Few Words More). AR

June 15 to August 15: Under the general title "Réflexions sur quelques-uns de mes contemporains" (Reflections on a Few of My Contemporaries), the following articles in the *Revue Fantaisiste*:

June 15: "I. Victor Hugo." AR

July 1: "II. Marceline Desbordes-Valmore." AR

July 15: "III. Auguste Barbier"; "IV. Théophile Gautier"; "V. Pétrus Borel." AR

August 1: "VI. Gustave Le Vavasseur"; "VII. Théodore de Banville." AR

August 15: "VIII. Pierre Dupont"; "IX. Leconte de Lisle." AR

September 15: "Peintures murales d'Eugène Delacroix à Saint-Sulpice" (Eugene Delacroix's Murals at Saint-Sulpice), *Revue Fantaisiste.* AR

September 15: **La Prière d'un païen** (The Prayer of a Pagan), **Le Rebelle** (The Rebel), **L'Avertisseur** (The One Who Warns), **Épigraphe pour un livre condamné** (Epigraph for a condemned book), *Revue Européenne.* FM

October 15: "Les Martyrs ridicules, par Léon Cladel" (The Ludicrous Martyrs, by Léon Cladel), review, *Revue Fantaisiste.* AR

November 1: **Recueillement** (Meditation), *Revue Européenne.* FM

November 1: Under the overall title "Poëmes en prose" (Poems in Prose), nine pieces, of which three were previously unpublished: **Les Foules** (The Crowds), **Les Veuves** (The Widows), **Le vieux Saltimbanque** (The Ancient Clown), *Revue Fantaisiste.* PPP

1862

January 12: Seven poems, of which two were previously unpublished: **Le Couvercle** (The Lid), **Le Coucher du soleil romantique** (The Sunset of the Romantic), *Le Boulevard.* FM

Second half of January: "Une réforme à l'Académie" (A Reform at the Academy), anonymous, *Revue Anecdotique.* OP, I

March 1: **Le Gouffre** (The Gulf), **La Lune offensée** (The Offended Moon), reprint of **La Voix** (The Voice), *L'Artiste.* FM

Second half of March: article on Paul de Molènes, without title, anonymous, *Revue Anecdotique.* OP, I

Second half of April: "L'Eau-forte est à la mode" (Etching is in

Fashion), anonymous. This was the first draft of "Peintres et aquafortistes" (Painters and Etchers), *Revue Anecdotique.* AR

April 20: "Les Misérables, par Victor Hugo" (Les Misérables, by Victor Hugo), review, *Le Boulevard.* AR

July 12, 19, and 26, August 2: "Le Joueur d'échecs de Maelzel" (translation of "Maelzel's Chess-Player"), *Le Monde Illustré.* HGS

August 26 and 27, September 24: under the overall title "Petits poëmes en prose" (Little Poems in Prose), the dedication to Arsène Houssaye, and the first twenty poems from the posthumous collection of the same title, were printed in *La Presse.* Of these, fourteen were previously unpublished, as follows:

August 26: **L'Étrange** (The Stranger), **Le Désespoir de la Vieille** (The Despair of the Old Woman), **Le Confiteor de l'artiste** (The Artist's Confiteor), **Un Plaisant** (A Jester), **La Chambre double** (The Double Room), **Chacun la sienne** (Everyone Hers), **Le Fou et la Vénus** (The Fool and Venus), **Le Chien et le Flacon** (The Dog and the Flask), **Le Mauvais Vitrier** (The Wicked Glazier). PPP

August 27: **A une heure du matin** (At One O'Clock in the Morning), **La Femme sauvage et la petite maîtresse** (The Wild Woman and Her Little Mistress). PPP

September 24: **Le Gâteau** (The Cake), **Le Joujou du Pauvre** (The Poor Man's Playthings), **Les Dons des Fées** (The Fairies' Gifts). PPP

September 14: "Peintures et aquafortistes" (Painters and Etchers), *Le Boulevard.* AR

December 28: **La Plainte d'un Icare** [Les Plaintes d'un Icare] (The Lament of an Icarus; also titled The Laments . . .), *Le Boulevard.* FM

1863

January 25: **L'Imprévu** (The Unforeseen), *Le Boulevard.* FM

Feburary 1: **L'Examen de minuit** (The Examination of Conscience at Midnight), *Le Boulevard.* FM

June 10: under the overall title "Petit poëmes en prose": **Les Tentations ou Éros, Plutus et la Gloire** (The Temptations or Eros, Plutus and Glory), **La Belle Dorothée** (The Beautiful Dorothy), *Revue Nationale et Etrangère.* PPP

June 14: under the title "Poëmes en prose": I, without a title, later called **Les Bienfaits de la Lune** (The Good Deeds of the Moon), and II, **Laquelle est la vraie?** (Which is the Real One?), *Le Boulevard.* PPP

October: **Lola de Valence,** *La Société des Aquafortistes,* October issue. FM

September 2 and 14, November 22: "L'Œuvre et la vie d'Eugène Delacroix" (The Life and Work of Eugene Delacroix), *L'Opinion Nationale.* AR

October 10: under the title "Petits poëmes en prose": **I, Une mort héroïque** (A Heroic Death), II, **Le Désir de peindre** (The Desire to Paint), *Revue Nationale et Étrangère.* PPP

Ca. November 25: Reprint of *Eurêka* (translation), Michel Lévy, Paris, 1864, 248pp. E

November 26 and 28, December 3: "Le Peintre de la vie moderne" (The Painter of Modern Life), *Figaro.* AR

December 10: under the title "Petits poëmes en prose: **Le Thyrse (A Franz Liszt)** (The Thyrsus: For Franz Liszt), **Les Fenêtres** (The Windows), **Déjà** (Already), *Revue Nationale et Étrangère.* PPP

1864

February 7: under the title "Le Spleen de Paris, Poëmes en prose" (The Spleen of Paris: Poems in Prose): **La Corde (A Édouard Manet)** (The Rope: For Edward Manet), reprint of **Le Crépuscule du soir** (Evening Twilight), **Le Joueur généreux** (The Generous Gambler), **Enivrez-vous** (Get Drunk), *Revue Nationale et Étrangère.* PPP

February 14: under the title "Le Spleen de Paris, Poëmes en prose": **Les Vocations** (Vocations), **Un cheval de race** (A Thoroughbred Horse), *Revue Nationale et Étrangère.* PPP

March 1: **Les Yeux de Berthe** (Bertha's Eyes), reprint of **Le**

Gouffre (The Gulf), **Sur "Le Tasse en prison" d'Eugène Delacroix** (On the Painting *Tasso in Prison,* by Eugène Delacroix), **Bien loin d'ici** (Ever so Far From Here), *Revue Nouvelle.* FM

April 14: "Anniversaire de la naissance de Shakespeare" (Anniversary of the Birth of Shakespeare), anonymous, *Figaro.* OP, I

April 24: "Vente de la collection de M. Eugène Piot" (Sale of Mr. Eugene Piot's Collection), *Figaro.* OP, II

July 2: **Les Yeux des pauvres** (The Eyes of the Poor), *La Vie Parisienne.* PPP

October 1: **Sur les débuts de Mademoiselle Amina Boschetti** (On the Debuts of Mademoiselle Amina Boschetti), *La Vie Parisienne.* FM

November 1: under the title "Petits poëmes en prose," three pieces, one of which was previously unpublished: **La Fausse Monnaie** (The False Money), *L'Artiste.* PPP

December 25: under the title "Le Spleen de Paris, Poëmes en prose": six pieces, of which two were previously unpublished: **Le Port** (The Harbor), **Le Miroir** (The Mirror), *Revue de Paris.* PPP

1865

January 7, 14, 21 and 28: "Le Système du docteur Goudron et du Professeur Plume" (translation of "The System of Doctor Tarr and Professor Fether"), *Le Monde Illustré.* HGS

March 16: *Histoires grotesques et sérieuses* (Grotesque and Serious Stories: translations), Michel Lévy, Paris, 1865, 372 pp. This volume contained two previously unpublished pieces: "Le Mystère de Marie Roget" (translation of "The Mystery of Marie Roget"), and "Le Domaine d'Arnheim" (translation of "The Domain of Arnheim, or The Landscape Garden"), **Le Cottage Landor.**

June 21: **Les Bons Chiens (A M. Joseph Stevens)** (The Good Dogs: For Mr. Joseph Stevens), *Indépendance Belge.* PPP

July 8: **Le Jet d'eau** (The Spurt of Water), *La Petite Revue.* FM

October 28: "Le comédien Rouvière" (The Comedian Rouviere), obituary note, signed C. B., *La Petite Revue*. AR

October: **Vers pour le portrait de M. Honoré Daumier** (Poem for the Portrait of Honore Daumier), in *Histoire de la caricature moderne* (A History of Modern Caricature) by Champfleury, Dentu, Paris, n.d. (1865).

1866

End of February, or beginning of March: *Les Épaves* (Waifs), at the Sign of the Rooster, Amsterdam [Poulet-Malassis, Brussels], 1866, 164pp., 260 copies, containing 23 poems, of which four were previously unpublished: under the subtitle "Galanteries" (Gallantries), **Les Promesses d'un visage** (The Promises of a Face), **Le Monstre ou le paranymphe d'une nymphe macabre** (The Monster), and under the subtitle "Bouffonneries" (Buffooneries), **A propos d'un importun** (With Regard to an Inopportune Man), **Un Cabaret folâtre** (A Wanton Tavern). FM

1867

September 21: **Portraits de maîtresses** (Portraits of Mistresses), *Revue Nationale et Étrangère*. PPP

September 28: **"Anywhere out of the world" N'importe où hors du monde**, *Revue Nationale et Étrangère*. PPP

October 11: **Le Tir et le Cimetière** (The Shooting and the Cemetery) *Revue Nationale et Étrangère*. PPP

Appendix

Posthumous edition of the complete works of Baudelaire, edited by Banville and Asselineau, for the publishing firm of Michel Lévy was as follows:

1868

I. *Les Fleurs du Mal* (dated 1869 on the cover), 411pp., containing 151 poems, of which only one was previously unpublished, **A Théodore de Banville** (To Theodore de Banville).

II. *Curiosités esthétiques* (dated 1869 on the cover), 440pp., containing nothing previously unpublished.

1869

III. *L'Art romantique,* (dated 1868 on the titlepage), 442pp., containing two previously unpublished essays, "L'Art philosophique" (Philosophic Art), and a study on "Hégésippe Moreau" written for the anthology *Les Poëtes français* (French Poets), edited by Eugene Crépet. This essay was refused by Crépet, doubtless for political reasons.

IV. *Petits poëmes en prose. Les Paradis artificiels,* 471pp. There are 50 prose poems, of which five were previously unpublished: **Le Galant Tireur** (The Gallant Rifleman), **La Soupe et les Nuages** (The Soup and the Clouds), **Perte d'Auréole** (The Loss of a Halo), **Mademoiselle Bistouri,** (Mademoiselle Bistouri), **Assommons les pauvres** (Down with the Poor!). The **Epilogue,** in verse, was also unpublished.

V. *Histoires extraordinaires.*

VI. *Nouvelles Histoires extraordinaires.*

1870

VII. *Aventures d'Arthur Gordon Pym—Eurêka.*

II. CRITICAL EDITIONS

There is only one complete edition of the works of Baudelaire: it is the Conard edition, edited by Jacques Crépet, with the collaboration, in the last volumes, of Claude Pichois. This edition unites elegance of appearance with exactitude in the establishment of the correct text. It contains extensive information. It comprises nineteen volumes, of which three are devoted to the posthumous works, six to correspondence, and five to translation. The edition was published from 1922 to 1953.

There is only one thing that is regrettable in this entire work: that is the use of the posthumous edition for the text of *Les Fleurs du Mal.* Jacques Crépet corrected this error himself in his monumental critical edition of *Les Fleurs du Mal* in 1942, which he prepared in collaboration with Georges Blin, and published with the firm of José Corti. For this edition, he took the text of 1861 as his starting-point. Later, in 1949, Crépet and Blin prepared a critical edition of *Journaux intimes* for the same firm. This work was equally noteworthy.

The edition undertaken by the *Nouvelle Revue Française* in 1918 raised the highest hopes: beautiful appearance, and a competence which seemed to offer every guarantee for a fine edition. Unfortunately, at that time Baudelairean scholarship was not sufficiently advanced, and this resulted in grave omissions. Besides, the first publisher of this edition, Félix Gautier, who was remarkably well-informed for his time, lacked the discipline necessary for a work of this kind. His first volume of *Fleurs du Mal* remains significant, however, for in it he reproduced the text of the first edition, followed by successive additions in the order in which they were produced. Even here, the accuracy of this edition is open to question. Moreover, this edition, which, in spite of the efforts of Le Dantec, remains incomplete, was limited to a mere 1200 copies.

The handiest edition of Baudelaire is that which the same Le Dantec edited for the Bibliothèque de la Pléiade. The first two volumes have now been bound as one. If we add to that a volume of the translations, we have, in two volumes, all of the essential work of Baudelaire, together with a precise and useful bibliography and a few notes.

Also noteworthy is the remarkable edition of the Club du Meilleur Livre, Coll. "Le Nombre d'or," 2 vol., 1955, which contains a wealth of commentaries and documents.

III. WORKS ON BAUDELAIRE

Much has been written on Baudelaire, but the truly valuable books are few. As far as his biography is concerned, the basic work remains that of Eugene Crépet, which first appeared in 1887, but is still more valuable in its later, definitive edition: *Charles Baudelaire, étude biographique d'Eugène Crépet, revue et mise à jour par Jacques Crépet, suivie des Baudelairiana d'Asselineau,* Leon Vanier, Messein, Succr., Paris, 1906. This work has been recently reprinted.

There is also much to be gained from a perusal of the works listed below in chronological order.

R. Pincebourde, ed. *Charles Baudelaire, Souvenirs—Correspondances—Bibliographie*. Paris, 1872.

Champfleury. *Souvenirs et portraits de jeunesse*. Dentu, 1872. (Chapter 23.)

M. Barrès. "La Folie de Charles Baudelaire," *Les Taches d'encre*, Nov. and Dec. 1884, and as a pamphlet issued by Les Ecrivains réunis, n.d. (1926).

A. Cassagne. *Versification et métrique de Baudelaire*. Hachette, 1906.

J. Laforgue. Notes in *Mélanges posthumes*. Mercure de France, 1909.

F. Nadar. *Charles Baudelaire intime*. Blaizot, 1911.

Gonzague de Reynold. *Charles Baudelaire*. Cres, 1920.

M. Proust. "A propos de Baudelaire," *Nouvelle Revue Française*, June 1921; reprinted in *Chroniques*, Gallimard, 1927.

E. Raynaud. *Charles Baudelaire*. Garnier, 1922.

P. Valéry. "Situation de Baudelaire," *Revue de France*, 15 Sept. 1924; reprinted in *Variété II*, Gallimard, 1930.

St. Fumet. *Notre Baudelaire*. Plon, 1926.

R. Vivier. *L'Originalité de Baudelaire*. Brussels and Paris, Renaissance de Livre, 1926; reprinted 1952.

L. Lemonnier. *Enquêtes sur Baudelaire*. Crès, 1929.

G. T. Clapton. "Balzac, Baudelaire and Maturin," *The French Quarterly*, 1930, pp. 66–84 and 97–115.

J. Pommier. *La Mystique de Baudelaire*. Les Belles-Lettres, 1932.

E. Starkie. *Baudelaire*. London, 1933; reprinted 1957.

A. Ferran. *L'Esthétique de Baudelaire*. Hachette, 1933.

W. T. Bandy. *Baudelaire judged by his contemporaries (1845–1867)*. New York, Publications of the Institute of French Studies, 1933.

R. Hughes. "Baudelaire et Balzac," *Mercure de France*, November 1934.

J. Charpentier. *Baudelaire*. Tallandier, 1937.

M. Seguin. *Génie des "Fleurs du Mal."* Messein, 1938.

G. Blin. *Baudelaire*. Gallimard, 1939.

M. Raymond. *De Baudelaire au Surréalisme*. José Corti, 1940.

F. Porché. *Baudelaire et la Présidente*. Geneva, 1941.

A. Feuillerat. *Baudelaire et la Belle aux cheveux d'or.* New Haven, Yale University Press, and Paris, José Corti, 1941.

A. Tabarant. *La Vie artistique au temps de Baudelaire.* Mercure de France, 1942.

F. Porché. *Baudelaire, histoire d'une âme.* Flammarion, 1945.

J. Mouquet and W. T. Bandy. *Baudelaire en 1848.* Émile-Paul, 1946.

B. Fondane. *Baudelaire et l'expérience du gouffre.* Seghers, 1947.

G. Blin. *Le Sadisme de Baudelaire.* José Corti, 1948.

J. Pommier. *Dans les chemins de Baudelaire.* José Corti, 1948.

H. Peyre. *Connaissance de Baudelaire.* José Corti, 1951.

J. Prévost. *Baudelaire, essai sur l'inspiration et la création poétiques,* Mercure de France, 1953.

J. Crépet and Cl. Pichois. *Baudelaire et Asselineau.* Nizet, 1953.

M. A. Ruff. *L'Esprit du Mal et l'esthétique baudelairienne.* A. Colin, 1955.

W. T. Bandy and Cl. Pichois. *Baudelaire devant ses contemporains.* Ed. du Rocher, 1957.

INDEX

For titles of Baudelaire's works, including translations and unrealized projects *see* Baudelaire, Charles: works

THE GOTHAM LIBRARY

Oscar Cargill, General Editor

Robert J. Clements, Associate Editor for Modern Languages

A paperback series devoted to major figures in world literature and topics of enduring importance

The Art of Paul Verlaine *by Antoine Adam (translated by Carl Morse)* $1.95

Shakespeare's Life and Art *by Peter Alexander* $1.95

Gabriela Mistral: The Poet and Her Work *by Margot Arce de Vázquez (translated by Helene Masslo Anderson)* $1.75

The Literary Reputation of Hemingway in Europe *edited by Roger Asselineau* $1.95

The Literary Origins of Surrealism: A New Mysticism in French Poetry *by Anna Balakian* $1.75

Borges the Labyrinth Maker *by Ana María Barrenechea (translated by Robert Lima)* $1.95

Madame Bovary and the Critics: A Collection of Essays *edited by B. F. Bart* $2.25

The Landscape of Nightmare: Studies in the Contemporary American Novel *by Jonathan Baumbach* $1.95

The Importance of Scrutiny *edited by Eric Bentley* $2.25

Balzac and the Human Comedy *by Philippe Bertault (English version by Richard Monges)* $2.25

Virginia Woolf *by Dorothy Brewster* $1.75

Passages from the Prose Writings of Matthew Arnold *edited by William F. Buckler* $1.95

Stendhal *by Armand Caraccio (translated by Dolores Bagley)* $2.25

O'Neill and His Plays *edited by Oscar Cargill, N. Bryllion Fagin, and William J. Fisher* $2.95

The Poetry of Michelangelo *by Robert Clements* $3.95

The Imagination of Charles Dickens *by A. O. Cockshut* $1.95

The Stanislavsky Heritage: Its Contribution to the Russian and American Theatre *by Christine Edwards* $3.50

The Modern Spanish Novel *by Sherman H. Eoff* $1.95

Dante and His Comedy *by Allan Gilbert* $1.95

Kipling and the Critics *edited by Elliot L. Gilbert* $1.95

The Three Jameses *by C. Hartley Grattan* $2.75

A Critical History of Old English Literature *by Stanley B. Greenfield* $2.25